THE MOSAICS OF SAN MARCO IN VENICE

729.7
D399

v. 2/2

Otto Demus

THE MOSAICS OF SAN MARCO IN VENICE

2

The Thirteenth Century

Volume Two: Plates

Published for Dumbarton Oaks, Washington, D. C.

THE UNIVERSITY OF CHICAGO PRESS
CHICAGO AND LONDON

WITHDRAWN

160969

LIBRARY ST. MARY'S COLLEGE

Unless otherwise credited, all photographs are by Ekkehard Ritter.

The University of Chicago Press, Chicago 60637
The University of Chicago Press, Ltd., London
© 1984 by Dumbarton Oaks
All rights reserved. Published 1984
Printed and bound by Amilcare Pizzi, s.p.a., Milan, Italy
90 89 88 87 . 86 85 84   1 2 3 4 5

Publication of this work has been assisted by a grant from the
Publications Program of the National Endowment for the Humanities,
an independent federal agency.

LIBRARY OF CONGRESS CATALOGING IN PUBLICATION DATA

Demus, Otto.
  The mosaics of San Marco in Venice.

  Includes bibliographies and indexes.
  Contents: 1. The eleventh and twelfth centuries
(2 v.) — 2. The thirteenth century. v. 2, Plates.
  1. Mosaics, Medieval—Italy—Venice. 2. Mosaics—
Italy—Venice. I. Basilica di San Marco (Venice,
Italy). I. Title.
NA3788.D45   729',7'094531   82-2787
ISBN 0-226-14289-2

Color Plates

Black-and-White-Plates

COLOR PLATES

OR AT·ADQVOSMOX TENDI TET·EOSSVPHOCREPREHENDIT·┼

1 West arm, south wall: Agony in the Garden, central part

2 West arm, south wall: Agony in the Garden, kneeling Christ at left

3 West arm, south wall: Agony in the Garden, sleeping apostles at left

4 West arm, south wall: Agony in the Garden, Peter, Andrew, John

5 West arm, south wall: Agony in the Garden, standing Christ at left, head

6 West arm, south wall, Agony in the Garden, standing Christ at right, head

7 South transept: *Apparitio Sancti Marci*, Prayers for the Discovery of the Body

8 South transept: *Apparitio Sancti Marci*, Discovery of the Body

9 South transept: Prayers for the Discovery of the Body, group of bowing men at left, right section, busts

10 South transept: Prayers for the Discovery of the Body, group of bowing men at left, left section, busts

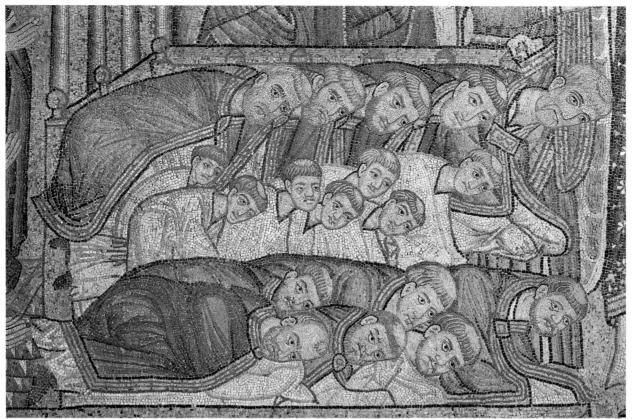

11 South transept: Prayers for the Discovery of the Body, clerics

12 South transept: Discovery of the Body, female figures at left, upper parts

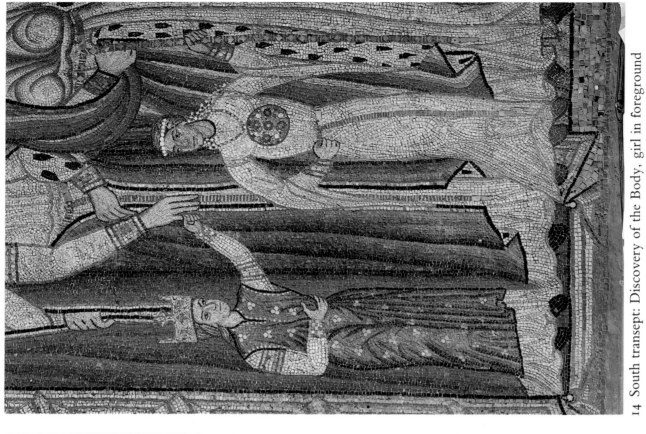

14 South transept: Discovery of the Body, girl in foreground

13 South transept: Discovery of the Body, female figures at left

15 South transept: Discovery of the Body, doge, councillors, heads

16 West arm, north wall: Christ Emmanuel

17 West arm, north wall: Christ Emmanuel, head

19 West arm, south wall: Solomon

18 West arm, south wall: Virgin

21 West arm, south wall: Ezekiel

20 West arm, north wall: Micah

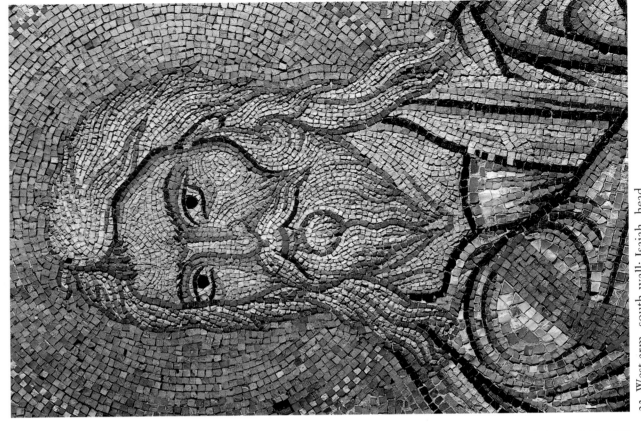

23 West arm, south wall: Isaiah, head

22 West arm, north wall: Jeremiah, head

25 Northwest pier of west dome: Paul Martyr, head

24 Northwest pier of west dome: Gerard, head

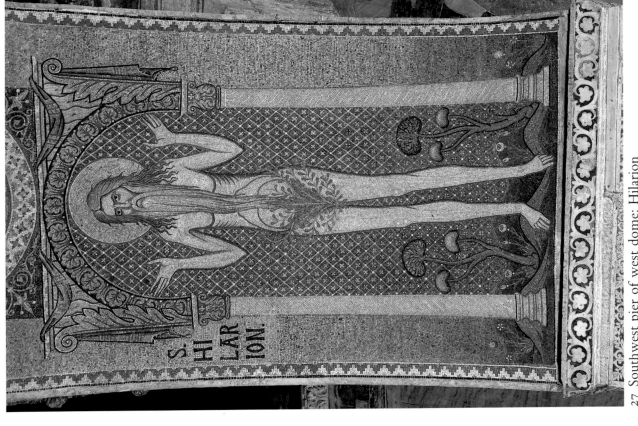

27 Southwest pier of west dome: Hilarion

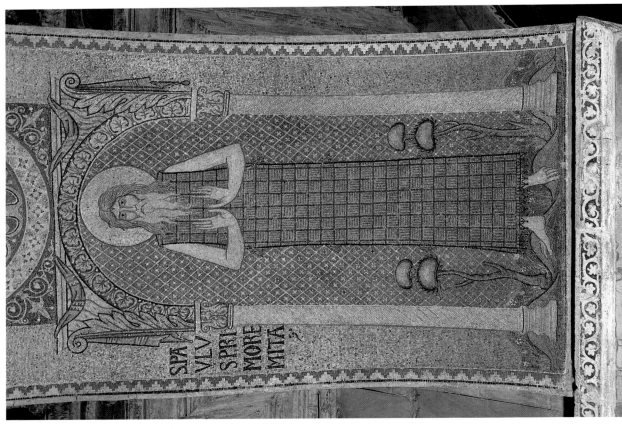

26 Southwest pier of west dome: Paul the Hermit

29 Northwest pier of central dome: Julian

28 Northwest pier of west dome: Paul Martyr

30 Atrium, Creation cupola: Separation of Light from Darkness, God

31 Atrium, Creation cupola: Creation of the Heavenly Bodies, left half

32 Atrium, Creation cupola: Expulsion

33 Atrium, Creation cupola: Creation of the Birds and Marine Creatures

35 Atrium, Creation cupola, northeast pendentive: cherub

34 Atrium, Creation cupola: Creation of Eve, Forming of Eve

37 Atrium, Creation cupola, southwest pendentive: cherub, head

36 Atrium, Creation cupola: Forming of Adam, God, head

39 Atrium, Creation cupola, south lunette: Wrath of Cain

38 Atrium, Creation cupola, east lunette: Begetting of Cain

40 Atrium, entrance bay, south vault: Noah, His Family, and the Animals Leaving the Ark, two figures at left, heads

41 Atrium, entrance bay, south vault: Noah Bringing Fowl into the Ark

42 Atrium, entrance bay, south vault: Noah, His Family, and the Animals Leaving the Ark

43 Atrium, entrance bay, north vault: Ham Seeing Noah Naked

45 Atrium, entrance bay, north vault: Burial of Noah, Noah, bust

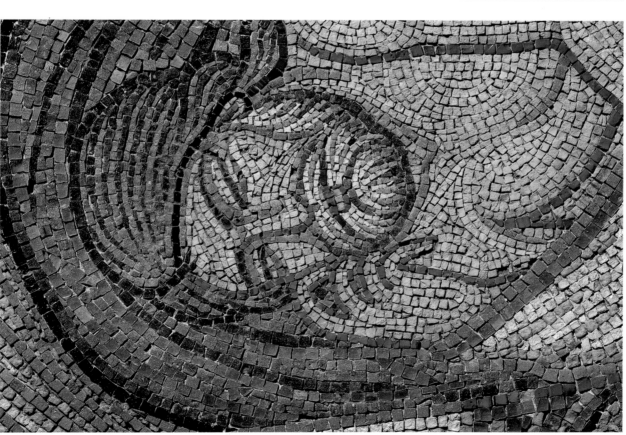

44 Atrium, entrance bay, north vault: Shem and Japheth Covering Noah, Noah, bust

47 Atrium, entrance bay, north vault: Appearance of the Lord at
Babel and the Confounding of the Languages, God, bust

46 Atrium, entrance bay, north vault: Appearance of the Lord at
Babel and the Confounding of the Languages, God, angels

48 Atrium, Abraham cupola, view from below

49 Atrium, Abraham cupola: Departure for Canaan

50 Atrium, Abraham cupola, west lunette: Birth of Isaac

51 Atrium, Abraham cupola, east lunette: Hospitality of Abraham, central section

52 Atrium, Abraham cupola: Departure for Canaan, Abraham, bust

53 Atrium, first Joseph cupola, view from below

54 Atrium, first Joseph cupola: Joseph Telling His Dream to His Father and Brethren

55 Atrium, first Joseph cupola: Joseph Thrown into the Pit and Brethren Feasting

56 Atrium, first Joseph cupola, west lunette: two birds at a fountain

57 Atrium, first Joseph cupola: Jacob Rending His Clothes, brethren at left, heads

58 Atrium, first Joseph cupola: Nathan

59 Atrium, second Joseph cupola, view from below

60 Atrium, second Joseph cupola: Potiphar's Wife Displays the Garment to the People of Her House

61 Atrium, second Joseph cupola: Pharaoh Throwing the Butler and the Baker into Prison

62 Atrium, second Joseph cupola: Butler Serving Pharaoh

63 Atrium, second Joseph cupola: Potiphar's Wife Displays the Garment to the People of Her House, witnesses, heads

64 Atrium, second Joseph cupola, south lunette: Pharaoh and the Egyptian Magicians, magicians, busts

66 Atrium, second Joseph cupola: Butler before Pharaoh, Pharaoh, head

65 Atrium, second Joseph cupola: Pharaoh Throwing the Butler and the Baker into Prison, Pharaoh, head

67 Atrium, third Joseph cupola, view from below

68 Atrium, third Joseph cupola: Joseph Gathering Corn, worker at right, bust

69 Atrium, third Joseph cupola: Joseph Selling Corn, Joseph and guards, busts

70 Atrium, third Joseph cupola: central medallion

71 Atrium, third Joseph cupola: Birth of Manasseh and Ephraim

72 Atrium, third Joseph cupola: John the Evangelist

73 Atrium, Moses cupola, view from below

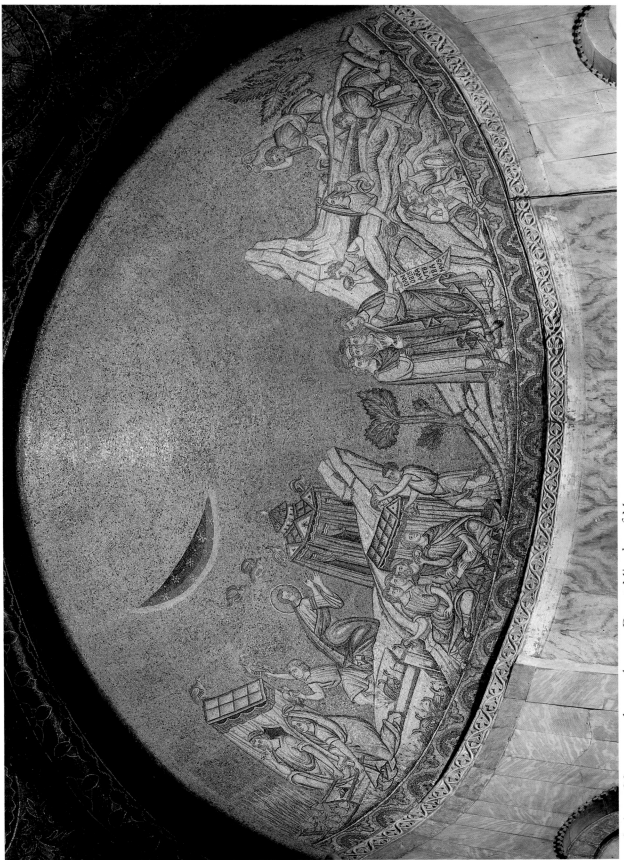

74 Atrium, Moses cupola, north apse: Desert Miracles of Moses

76 Atrium, Moses cupola: Moses Driving away the Shepherds,
Moses, head

75 Atrium, Moses cupola: Moses before Pharaoh

77 Atrium, Moses cupola: Moses and the Daughters of Jethro at the Well

78 Cappella Zen, vault, east half: Legend of Mark

BLACK-AND-WHITE PLATES

1a West arm, south wall: Agony in the Garden

1b West arm, south wall: Agony in the Garden

2 West arm, south wall: Agony in the Garden, sleeping apostles at left

3 West arm, south wall: Agony in the Garden, sleeping apostles, central section

5 West arm, south wall: Agony in the Garden, apostle, back row, left, head

4 West arm, south wall: Agony in the Garden, apostle, back row, second from left, head

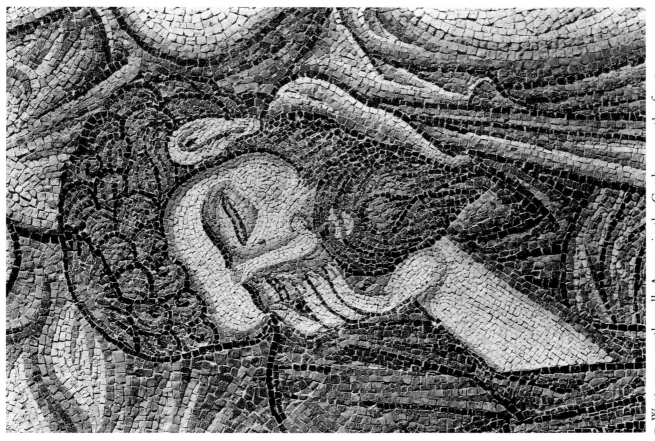

7 West arm, south wall: Agony in the Garden, apostle, front row, left, bust

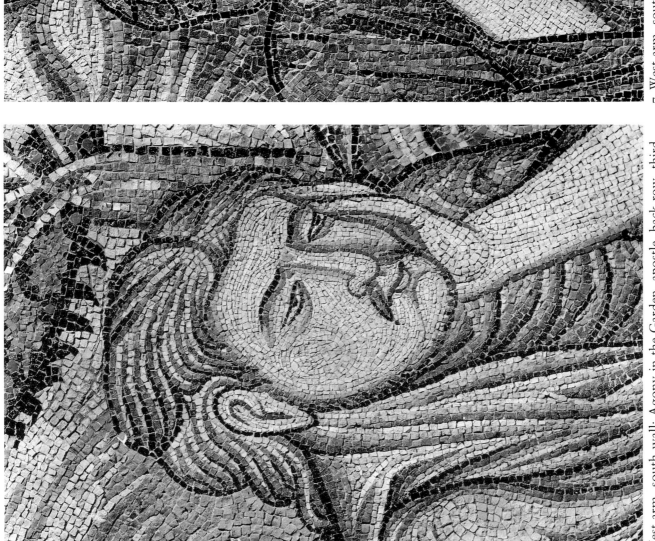

6 West arm, south wall: Agony in the Garden, apostle, back row, third from left, bust

9 West arm, south wall: Agony in the Garden, apostle, back row, fourth from left, head

8 West arm, south wall: Agony in the Garden, apostle, front row, third from left, head

11 West arm, south wall: Agony in the Garden, apostle, front row, third from left, head and upper body

10 West arm, south wall: Agony in the Garden, apostle, front row, second from left, head

13 West arm, south wall: Agony in the Garden, Andrew, head and upper body

12 West arm, south wall: Agony in the Garden, Peter at left, head

15 West arm, south wall: Agony in the Garden, kneeling Christ at left, head

14 West arm, south wall: Agony in the Garden, John, bust

17 West arm, south wall: Agony in the Garden, kneeling Christ at right

16 West arm, south wall: Agony in the Garden, standing Christ at left and apostles

19 West arm, south wall: Agony in the Garden, Peter at right, head and upper body

18 West arm, south wall: Agony in the Garden, Peter in center (*Strempel*)

21 West arm, south wall: Agony in the Garden, standing Christ at right, head

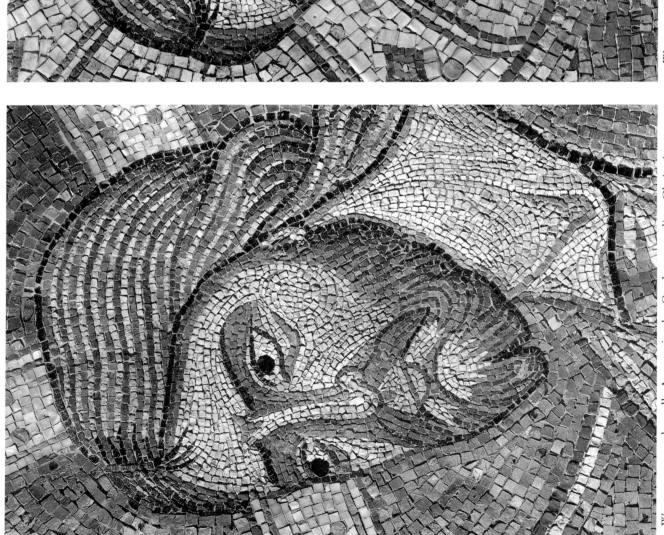

20 West arm, south wall: Agony in the Garden, standing Christ in center, head

23 West arm, south wall: Agony in the Garden, kneeling Christ at right, head

22 West arm, south wall: Agony in the Garden, kneeling Christ in center, head

LIBRARY ST. MARY'S COLLEGE

24 West arm, south wall: Agony in the Garden, kneeling Christ in center, hands

25 West arm, south wall: Agony in the Garden, standing Christ at left, feet and hem of garment

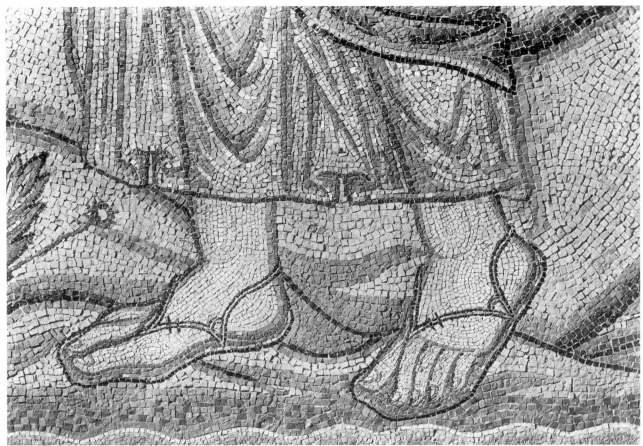

26 West arm, south wall: Agony in the Garden, standing Christ in center, feet and hem of garment

27 West arm, south wall: Agony in the Garden, standing Christ at right, feet and hem of garment

30 West arm, south wall: Agony in the Garden, tree below kneeling
Christ at left

28 West arm, south wall: Agony in the Garden, ornament, part of inscription
above scene

29 West arm, south wall: Agony in the Garden, angel

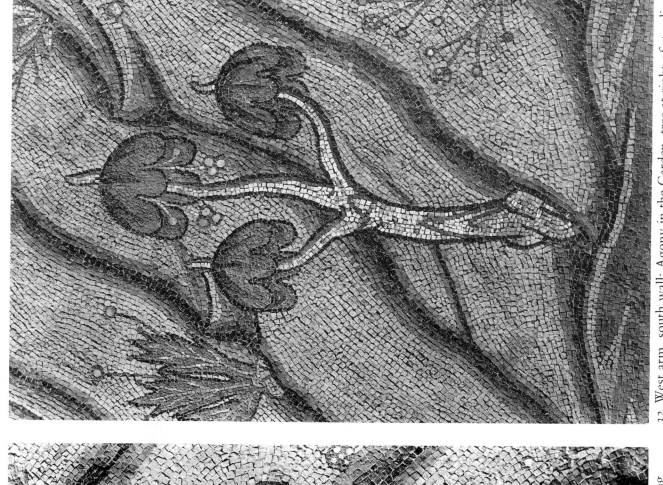

32 West arm, south wall: Agony in the Garden, tree at right of standing Christ in center

31 West arm, south wall: Agony in the Garden, tree below kneeling Christ in center

33 South transept: *Apparitio Sancti Marci, Prayers for the Discovery of the Body*

35 South transept: Prayers for the Discovery of the Body, kneeling figure fifth from left, head and hands

34 South transept: Prayers for the Discovery of the Body, woman at top left, head

36 South transept: Prayers for the Discovery of the Body, group of bowing men at left, left section, busts

37 South transept: Prayers for the Discovery of the Body, kneeling figures in foreground

38 South transept: Prayers for the Discovery of the Body, group of bowing men at left, right section, busts

39 South transept: Prayers for the Discovery of the Body, councillors, heads and upper bodies

40 South transept: Prayers for the Discovery of the Body, doge, head

41 South transept: Prayers for the Discovery of the Body, councillors, heads

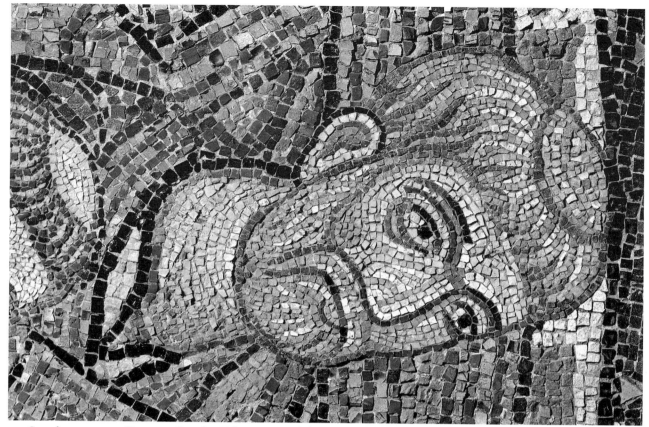

42 South transept: Prayers for the Discovery of the Body, cleric, top row, right, head

43 South transept: Prayers for the Discovery of the Body, clerics, top row, two figures at right, heads

44 South transept: Prayers for the Discovery of the Body, clerics, middle row, two figures at left, heads

45 South transept: Prayers for the Discovery of the Body, clerics, middle row, central section, heads

46 South transept: Prayers for the Discovery of the Body, clerics, front row, central section, heads

47 South transept: Prayers for the Discovery of the Body, cleric, front row, right, head

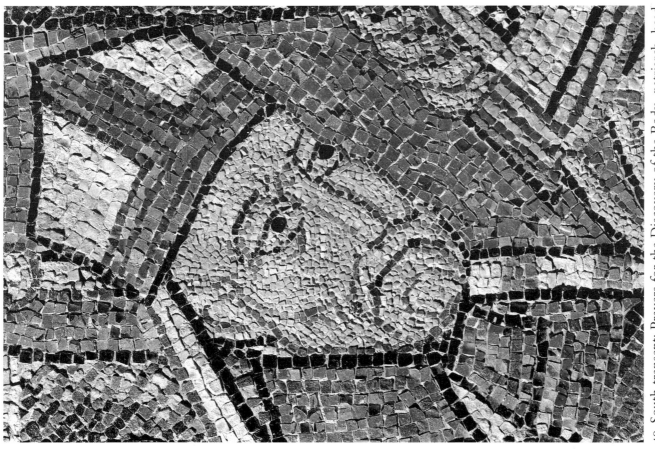

49 South transept: Prayers for the Discovery of the Body, patriarch, head

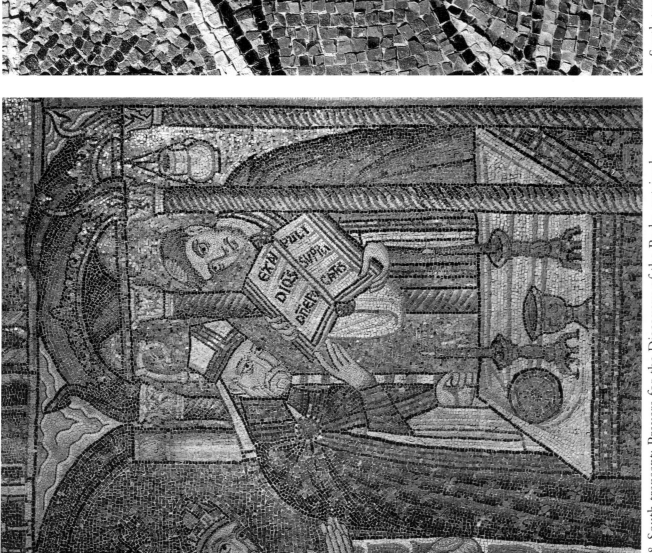

48 South transept: Prayers for the Discovery of the Body, patriarch, deacon, altar

50 South transept: *Apparitio Sancti Marci, Discovery of the Relics*

51 South transept: Discovery of the Relics, women at left, heads

52 South transept: Discovery of the Relics, women at left, right part, heads

53 South transept: Discovery of the Relics, men at left, heads

54 South transept: Discovery of the Relics, clerics, heads

56 South transept: Discovery of the Relics, girl in foreground, bust

55 South transept: Discovery of the Relics, prince, head

58 South transept: Discovery of the Relics, man at left, hands

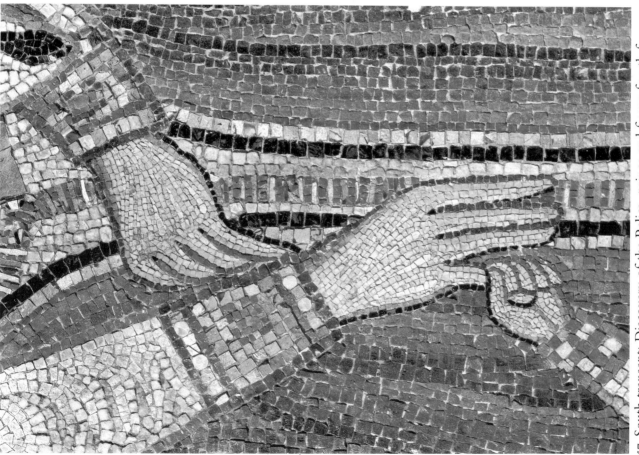

57 South transept: Discovery of the Relics, prince and figure fourth from left, hands

59 Northwest pier of central dome, cupola (Tribuna del Capitello), view looking east (*Böhm*)

60 West arm, north wall: Joel, Christ Emmanuel, Micah, Jeremiah

OSEE

QVASI OLV CVLVPPAT VS EST EG RESSVS E ? ET VENE TQ VASI VM BERNOBI MPORAN EVS ET SE ROTITE TRE

61 West arm, north wall: Hosea

63 West arm, north wall: Jeremiah

62 West arm, north wall: Joel (*Strempel*)

65 West arm, north wall: Joel, head

64 West arm, north wall: Hosea, head

67 West arm, north wall: Joel, left hand with scroll

66 West arm, north wall: Micah, head

69 West arm, north wall: Jeremiah, right hand

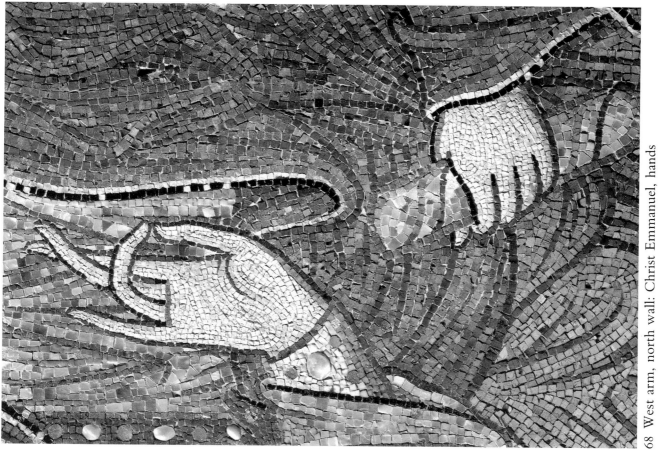

68 West arm, north wall: Christ Emmanuel, hands

DAVIO. PPHET̄A

·DEFR
VCTV
TERIS
TVIPONI
S̄VPSED
MEA·
:·

70 West arm, south wall: David

71 West arm, south wall: Isaiah

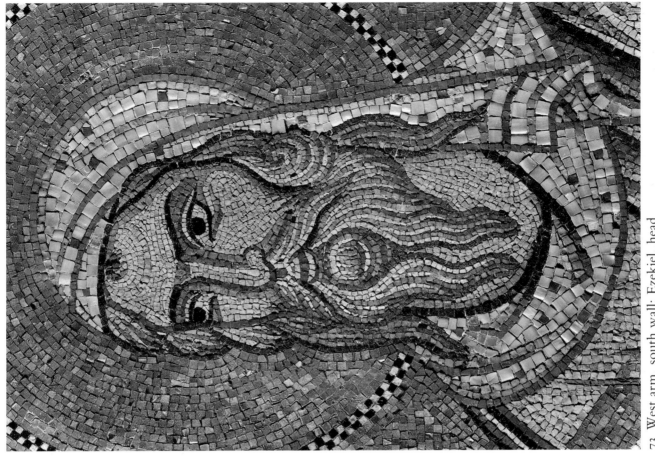

73 West arm, south wall: Ezekiel, head

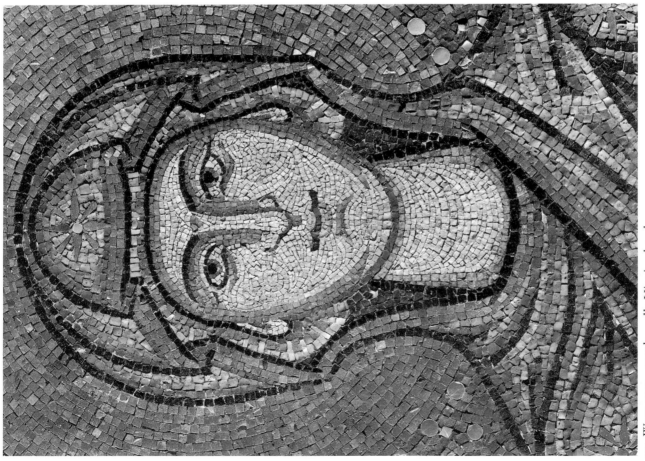

72 West arm, south wall: Virgin, head

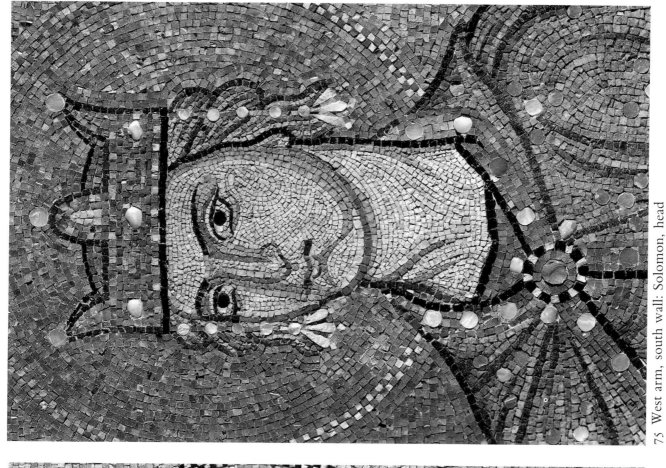

75 West arm, south wall: Solomon, head

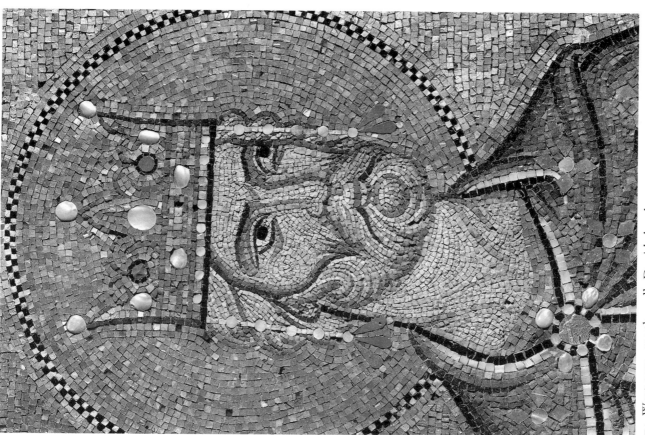

74 West arm, south wall: David, head

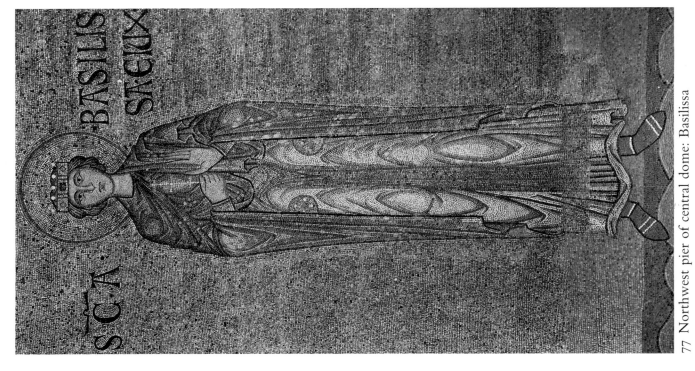

77 Northwest pier of central dome: Basilissa

76 Northwest pier of west dome: Gerard

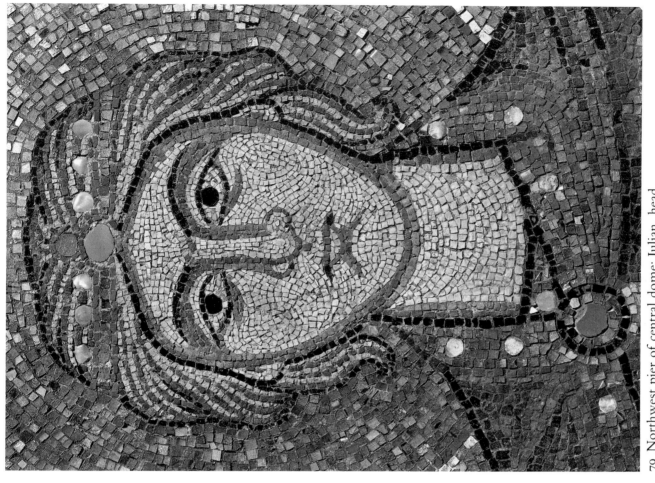

79 Northwest pier of central dome: Julian, head

78 Northwest pier of west dome: Paul Martyr, head

81 Northwest pier of central dome: Bassus, bust (*Procuratoria*)

80 Northwest pier of central dome: Bassus (*Böhm*)

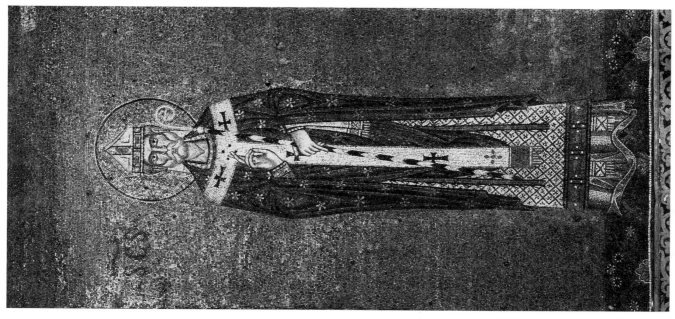

83 Southwest pier of central dome: anonymous saint (*Böhm*)

82 Northwest pier of central dome: Baldus (*Böhm*)

85 Southeast pier of central dome: Homobonus

84 Southeast pier of central dome: Boniface

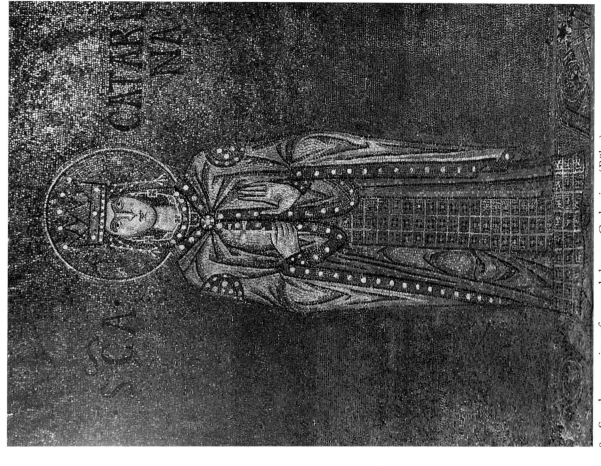

87 Southwest pier of central dome: Catherine (*Böhm*)

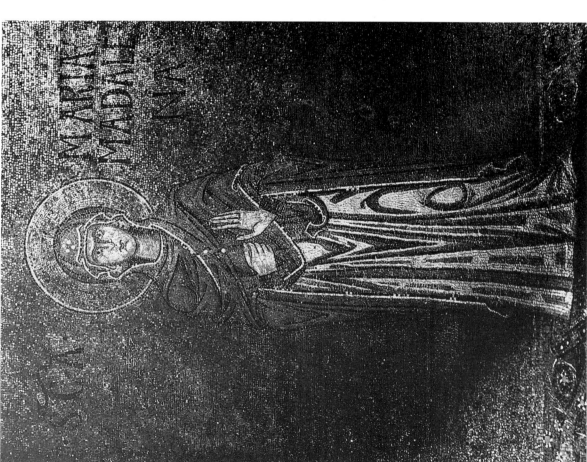

86 Southwest pier of central dome: Mary Magdalen (*Böhm*)

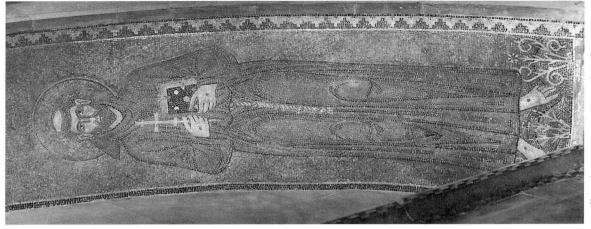

91 South transept: Francis of Assisi
(Böhm)

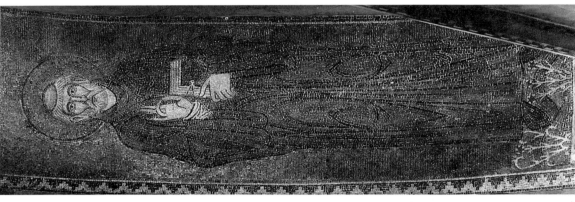

90 South transept: Benedict
(Böhm)

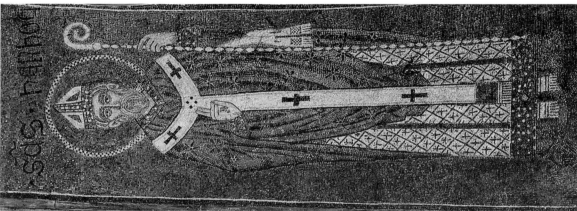

89 South transept: "Henhoc"
(Hermogenes?) (Böhm)

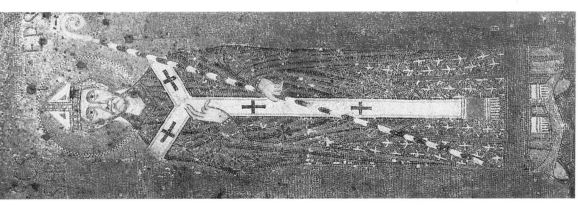

88 South transept: Sirus (Böhm)

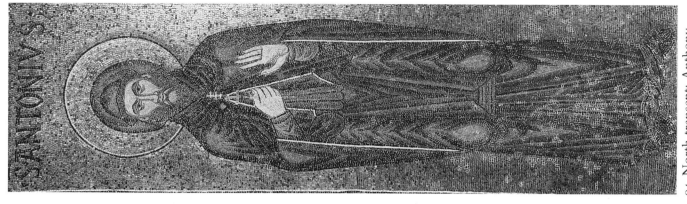

94 North transept: Anthony (*Böhm*)

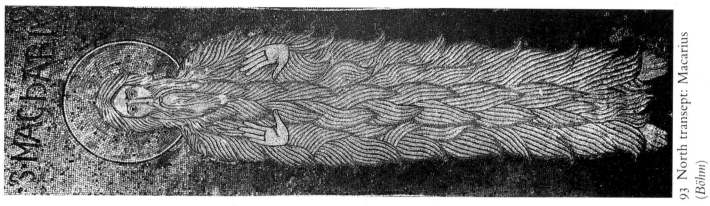

93 North transept: Macarius (*Böhm*)

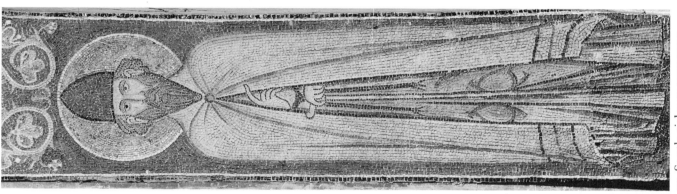

92 South aisle: anonymous saint (*Böhm*)

96 North transept: Anthony, head and upper body (*Böhm*)

95 South transept: Sirus, head and upper body (*Böhm*)

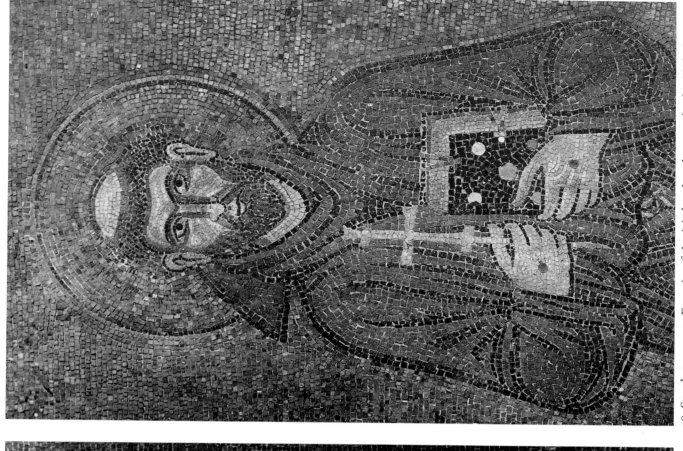

98 South transept: Francis of Assisi, head and upper body (*Böhm*)

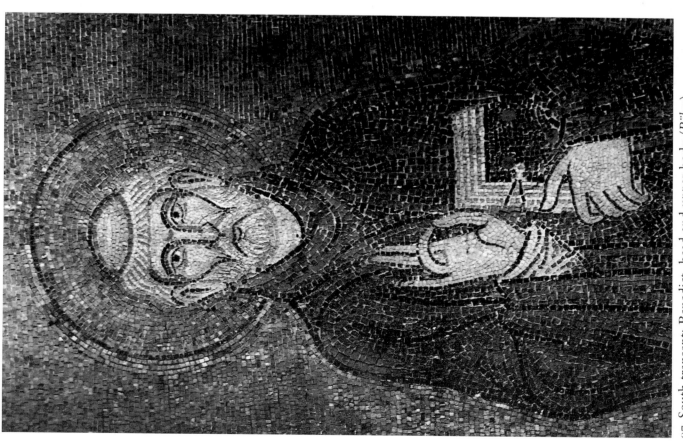

97 South transept: Benedict, head and upper body (*Böhm*)

99 Northwest pier of west dome, east arch soffit: apex ornament

100 Northwest pier of west dome, northwest corner: ornament

101 South transept, door to Treasury (Tesoro): angels (*Böhm*)

102 West door: lunette with Deesis (*Alinari*)

103 West door: lunette with Deesis, Christ, bust (*Procuratoria*)

105 West door: lunette with Deesis, Mark, bust (*Procuratoria*)

104 West door: lunette with Deesis, Virgin, bust (*Procuratoria*)

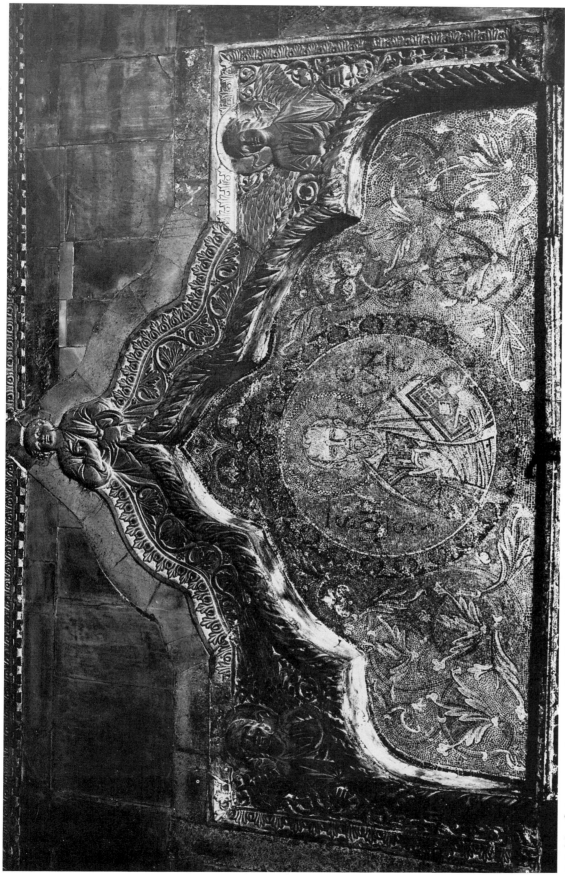

106 North transept, door to atrium (Porta San Giovanni): John (*Böhm*)

107 Atrium, Creation cupola, view from below (*Alinari*)

108 Atrium, Creation cupola: Spirit above the Waters

109 Atrium, Creation cupola: Separation of Light from Darkness

110 Atrium, Creation cupola: Creation of the Firmament

111 Atrium, Creation cupola: Separation of the Seas and the Dry Land

112 Atrium, Creation cupola: Creation of the Plants

113 Atrium, Creation cupola: Creation of the Heavenly Bodies

114 Atrium, Creation cupola: Blessing of the Birds and the Marine Creatures

115 Atrium, Creation cupola: Creation of the Terrestrial Animals

116 Atrium, Creation cupola: Forming of Adam

117 Atrium, Creation cupola: Blessing of the Seventh Day (*Böhm*)

118 Atrium, Creation cupola: Animation of Adam (*Böhm*)

119 Atrium, Creation cupola: Introduction of Adam into Paradise

120 Atrium, Creation cupola: Naming of the Animals

121 Atrium, Creation cupola: Creation of Eve

122 Atrium, Creation cupola: Introduction of Adam and Eve

123 Atrium, Creation cupola: Temptation of Eve

124 Atrium, Creation cupola: Eve Plucking Fruit and Giving It to Adam

125 Atrium, Creation cupola: Covering with Fig Leaves

126 Atrium, Creation cupola: Adam and Eve Hiding from the Presence of the Lord

127 Atrium, Creation cupola: Denial of Guilt

128 Atrium, Creation cupola: Punishment of Adam and the Curse of the Serpent

129 Atrium, Creation cupola: Clothing of Adam and Eve

130 Atrium, Creation cupola: Expulsion, Adam and Eve's Labor

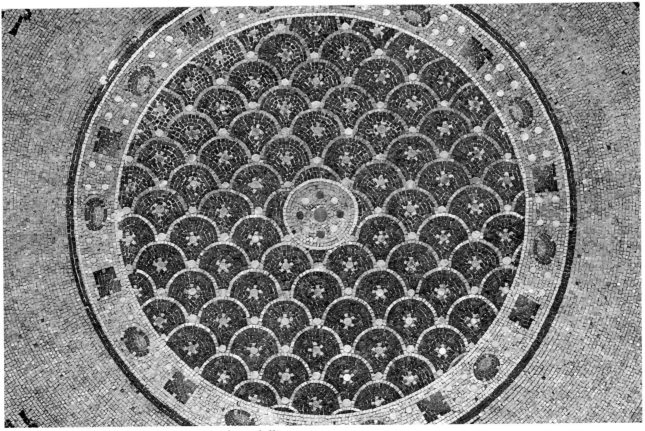

131 Atrium, Creation cupola: central medallion

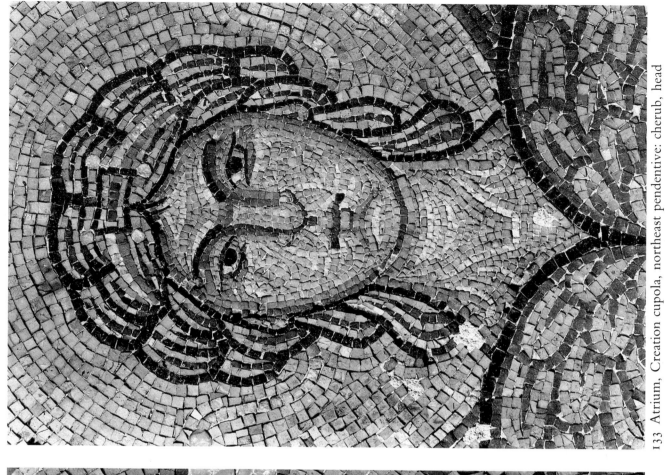

133 Atrium, Creation cupola, northeast pendentive: cherub, head

132 Atrium, Creation cupola: Naming of the Animals, God, head

134 Atrium, Creation cupola, east lunette (*Alinari*)

135 Atrium, Creation cupola, south lunette (*Böhm*)

136 Atrium, Creation cupola, east lunette: Birth of Abel (*Böhm*)

137 Atrium, Creation cupola, east lunette: Abel's Offering (*Böhm*)

138 Atrium, Creation cupola, east lunette: altar (*Böhm*)

139 Atrium, Creation cupola, east lunette, Cain's Offering (*Böhm*)

140 Atrium, Creation cupola, south lunette:
Wrath of Cain

141 Atrium, Creation cupola, south lunette:
Lord Speaking to Cain

142 Atrium, Creation cupola, south lunette:
Cain Talking to Abel (*Procuratoria*)

143 Atrium, Creation cupola, south lunette:
Cain Slaying Abel

144 Atrium, entrance bay, south vault, west half

FACTVQVEEOILVDIVPQVADRAGITADIEB;SVPRAETQVINDECICVBITISALCIORF
VITAQVASVPOMSMONTES,CVQ↑COSPRÉÉTOISCROSVPRÃEMISNOECOV
BÃ;

ATILLVENITADEVPORSRAMVOLREIORE·ETITELLEXNOE↑CESSASÉTRO·DILVII·
PONAMARCVINNVBIB;   ETERITSIGNVFEDERIS
                                     TROSITVLRA
                                     AQ
                                     VE
                                     OLL
                                     VV
                                     IV

NOEOPVLITHOLOCVSTVDRO·   PDLVVV·

145 Atrium, entrance bay, south vault, east half

146 Atrium, entrance bay, south vault: Building of the Ark, right section

148 Atrium, entrance bay, south vault: Building of the Ark, Noah, builder

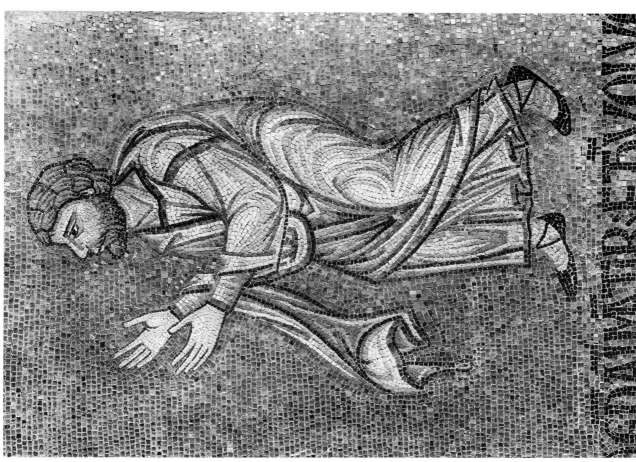

147 Atrium, entrance bay, south vault: Noah Ordered to Build the Ark, Noah

150 Atrium, entrance bay, south vault: Building of the Ark, workmen at right of upper sawyer, heads and upper bodies

149 Atrium, entrance bay, south vault: Building of the Ark, upper sawyer

151 Atrium, entrance bay, south vault: Noah Bringing Fowl into the Ark

152 Atrium, entrance bay, south vault: Noah Bringing the Terrestrial Animals into the Ark

153 Atrium, entrance bay, south vault: Noah Bringing His Family into the Ark

155 Atrium, entrance bay, south vault: Noah Bringing His Family into the Ark, Noah, eagles, ravens

154 Atrium, entrance bay, south vault: Noah Bringing the Terrestrial Animals into the Ark, Noah, lions

156 Atrium, entrance bay, south vault: Noah Bringing His Family into the Ark, birds at right

157 Atrium, entrance bay, south vault: Flood

158 Atrium, entrance bay, south vault: Noah Sending Forth the Raven and the First Dove

159 Atrium, entrance bay, south vault: Return of the Second Dove

160 Atrium, entrance bay, south vault: Noah Sending Forth the Raven and the First Dove, Noah, dove

161 Atrium, entrance bay, south vault: Noah, His Family, and the Animals Leaving the Ark

162 Atrium, entrance bay, south vault: Noah, His Family, and the Animals Leaving the Ark, lower half

163 Atrium, entrance bay, south vault: Noah, His Family, and the
Animals Leaving the Ark, Noah, lion

NOE O PTVLIT HOLOCAVSTV DÑO ·   · P DLVVIū·

164 Atrium, entrance bay, south vault: Sacrifice of Noah

166 Atrium, entrance bay, south vault: Noah Ordered to Build the Ark,
Noah, head

165 Atrium, entrance bay, south vault: Sacrifice of Noah, Noah, head

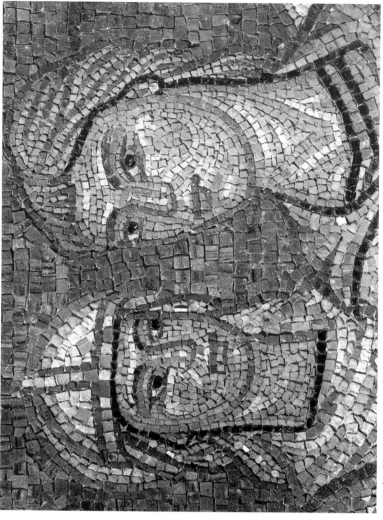

168 Atrium, entrance bay, south vault: Noah, His Family, and the Animals Leaving the Ark, figures third and fourth from left, heads

167 Atrium, entrance bay, south vault: Noah, His Family, and the Animals Leaving the Ark, woman at right, head

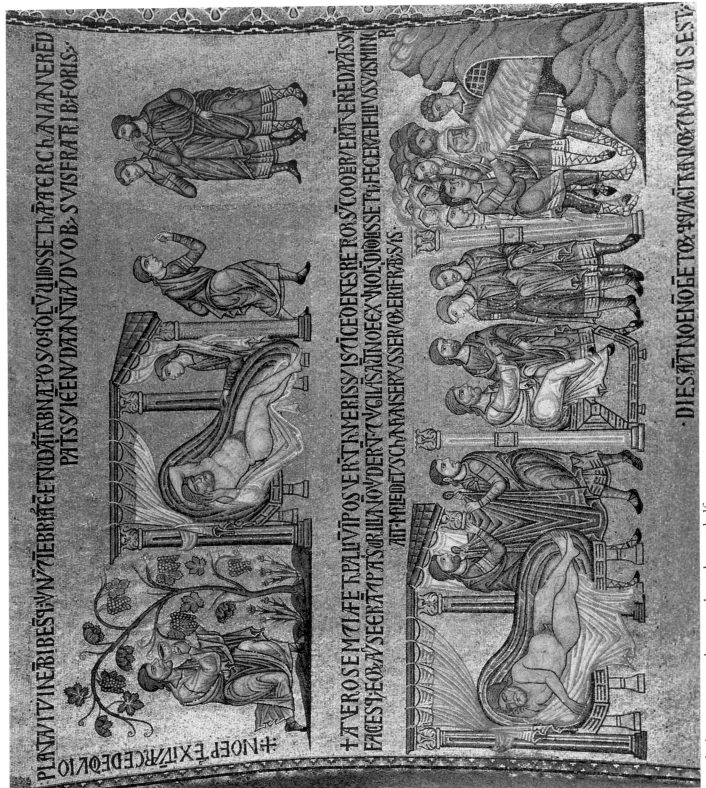

169 Atrium, entrance bay, north vault, east half

171 Atrium, entrance bay, north vault: Noah as Husbandman, Noah, bust

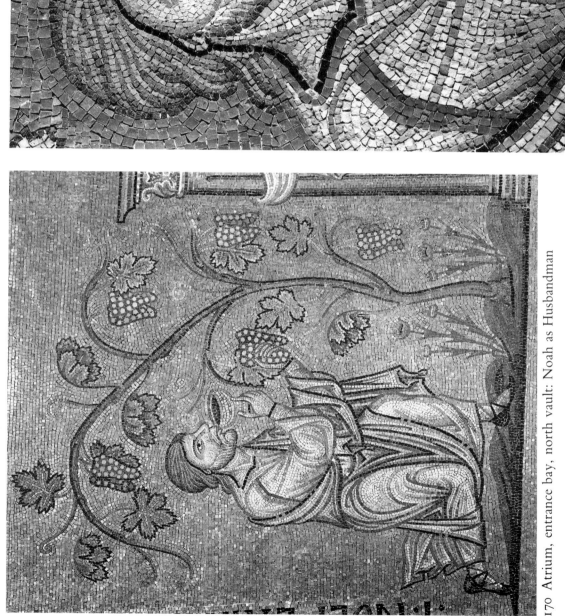

170 Atrium, entrance bay, north vault: Noah as Husbandman

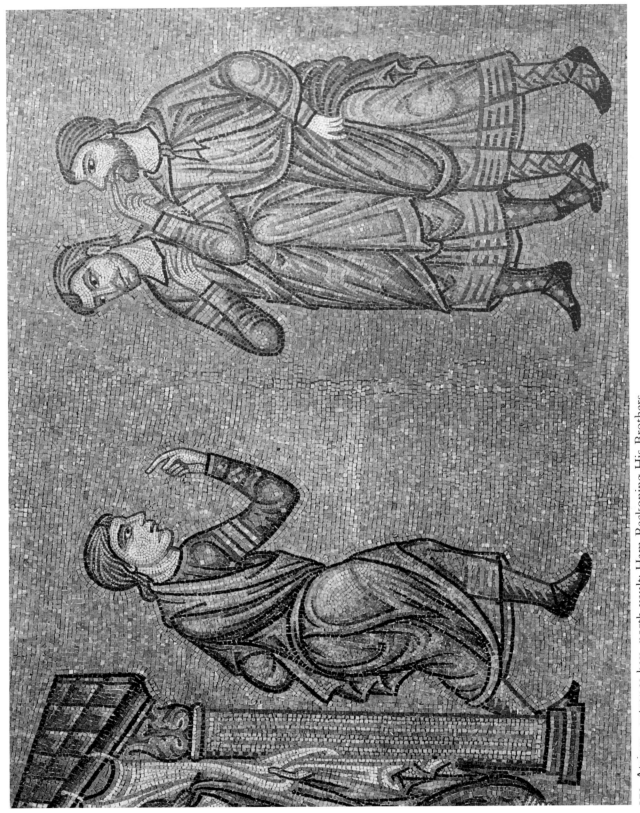

172 Atrium, entrance bay, north vault: Ham Beckoning His Brothers

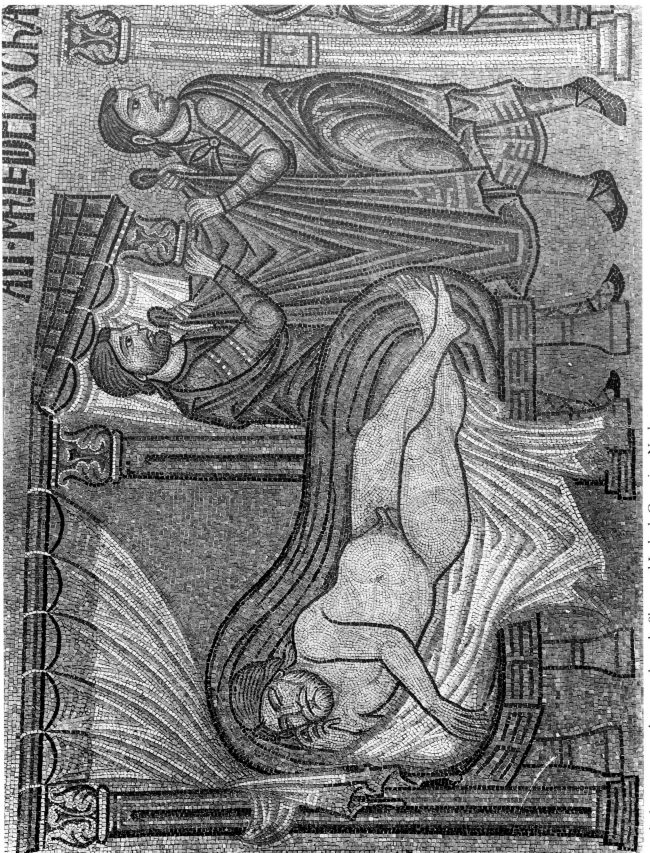

173 Atrium, entrance bay, north vault: Shem and Japheth Covering Noah

174 Atrium, entrance bay, north vault: Noah Cursing Canaan

175 Atrium, entrance bay, north vault: Burial of Noah

177 Atrium, entrance bay, north vault: Ham Beckoning His Brothers, Ham, head and upper body

176 Atrium, entrance bay, north vault: Ham Seeing Noah Naked, Noah, bust

179 Atrium, entrance bay, north vault: Burial of Noah, figure at right, head

178 Atrium, entrance bay, north vault: Noah Cursing Canaan, two figures at right, heads

180 Atrium, entrance bay, north vault, west half (*Alinari*)

181 Atrium, entrance bay, north vault: God, three angels

182 Atrium, entrance bay, north vault: Building of the Tower of Babel, group at right, heads and upper bodies

183 Atrium, entrance bay, north vault: Building of the Tower of Babel, standing figure at left

184 Atrium, entrance bay, north vault: Building of the Tower of Babel, figure climbing ladder

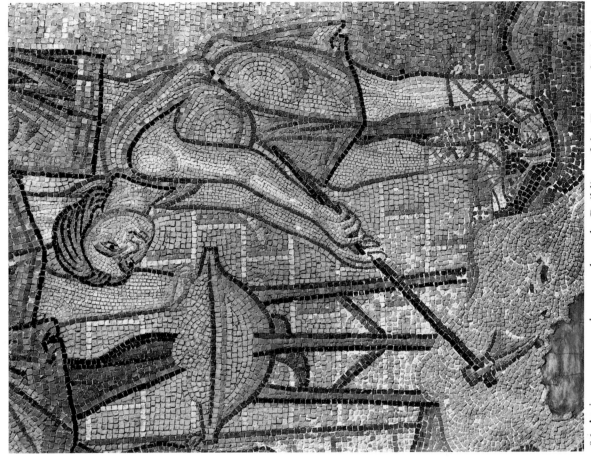

186 Atrium, entrance bay, north vault: Building of the Tower of Babel, figure at lower right

185 Atrium, entrance bay, north vault: Building of the Tower of Babel, figure at lower left

187 Atrium, entrance bay, north vault: Building of the Tower of Babel, figure at upper left

188 Atrium, entrance bay, north vault: Building of the Tower of Babel, figure at upper right

190 Atrium, entrance bay, north vault: Appearance of the Lord at Babel and the Confounding of the Languages, group at lower right

189 Atrium, entrance bay, north vault: Appearance of the Lord at Babel and the Confounding of the Languages, group at lower left

192 Atrium, entrance bay, north vault: Appearance of the Lord at Babel and the Confounding of the Languages, group at upper right

191 Atrium, entrance bay, north vault: Appearance of the Lord at Babel and the Confounding of the Languages, group at upper left

193 Atrium, Abraham cupola, view from below

194 Atrium, Abraham cupola: the Lord Speaking to Abraham and Departure to Canaan

195 Atrium, Abraham cupola: Departure to Canaan, upper part

196 Atrium, Abraham cupola: Departure to Canaan, man at right

197 Atrium, Abraham cupola: Journey to Canaan

198 Atrium, Abraham cupola: Journey to Canaan, Sarah and servants, busts

200 Atrium, Abraham cupola: Journey to Canaan, Lot, servants at right

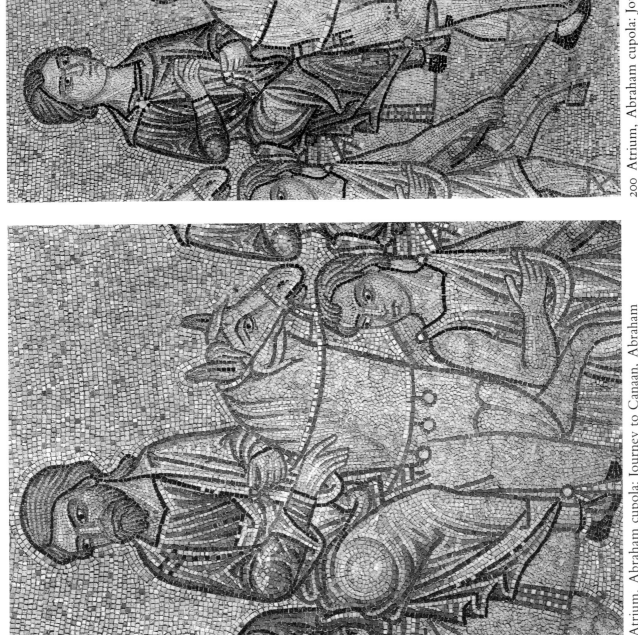

199 Atrium, Abraham cupola: Journey to Canaan, Abraham

202 Atrium, Abraham cupola: Journey to Canaan, Abraham, bust

201 Atrium, Abraham cupola: Journey to Canaan, Lot, bust

204 Atrium, Abraham cupola: Abraham Arming His Servants for the Liberation of Lot, Abraham, bust

203 Atrium, Abraham cupola: Abraham Arming His Servants for the Liberation of Lot

206 Atrium, Abraham cupola: Abraham Speaking with the Lord

205 Atrium, Abraham cupola: Departure to Canaan, Abraham, head and upper body

207 Atrium, Abraham cupola: Meeting of Abraham and Melchizedek, Men of Aner, Eshcol, and Mamre Taking Their Portion

208 Atrium, Abraham cupola: Men of Aner, Eshcol, and Mamre Taking Their Portion, Abraham and the King of Sodom

210 Atrium, Abraham cupola: Men of Aner, Eshcol, and Mamre Taking Their Portion

209 Atrium, Abraham cupola: Meeting of Abraham and Melchizedek, left upper section

212 Atrium, Abraham cupola: Meeting of Abraham and Melchizedek, Melchizedek, bust

211 Atrium, Abraham cupola: Meeting of Abraham and Melchizedek, Abraham, bust

213 Atrium, Abraham cupola: Abraham and the King of Sodom, the Lord's Covenant with Abraham

214 Atrium, Abraham cupola: the Lord's Covenant with Abraham, Abraham, head

215 Atrium, Abraham cupola: Hagar Given to Abraham, upper part

216 Atrium, Abraham cupola: Hagar Given to Abraham

217 Atrium, Abraham cupola: Abraham Handing Hagar over to Sarah

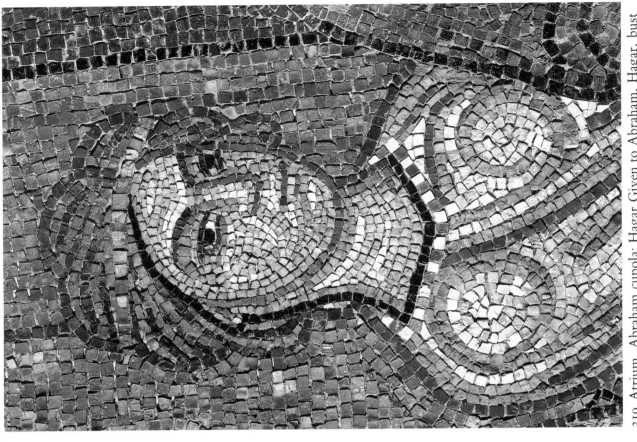

219 Atrium, Abraham cupola: Hagar Given to Abraham, Hagar, bust

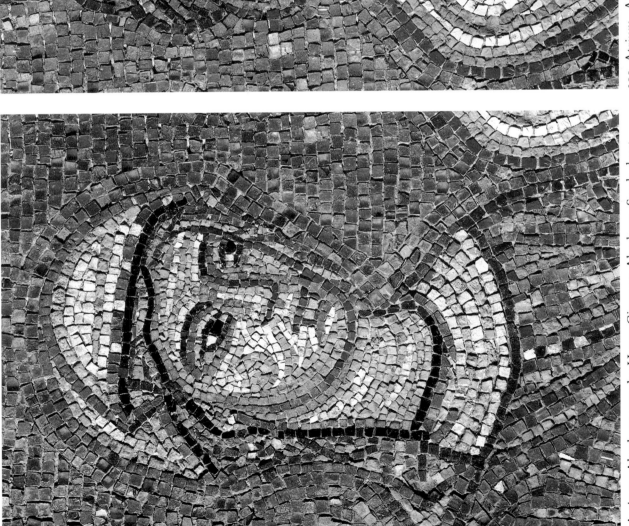

218 Atrium, Abraham cupola: Hagar Given to Abraham, Sarah, bust

221 Atrium, Abraham cupola: Abraham Handing Hagar over to Sarah, Hagar, bust

220 Atrium, Abraham cupola: Abraham Handing Hagar over to Sarah, Sarah, bust

222 Atrium, Abraham cupola: Birth of Ishmael, Lord Speaking to Abraham

223 Atrium, Abraham cupola: Discourse between Hagar and the Angel

LIBRARY ST. MARY'S COLLEGE

224 Atrium, Abraham cupola: Birth of Ishmael, Abraham, Sarah, busts

225 Atrium, Abraham cupola: Circumcision of Ishmael, women at right, busts

226 Atrium, Abraham cupola: Circumcision of Ishmael

227 Atrium, Abraham cupola. Circumcision of All the Men

228 Atrium, Abraham cupola: Circumcision of All the Men, Abraham, head and upper body

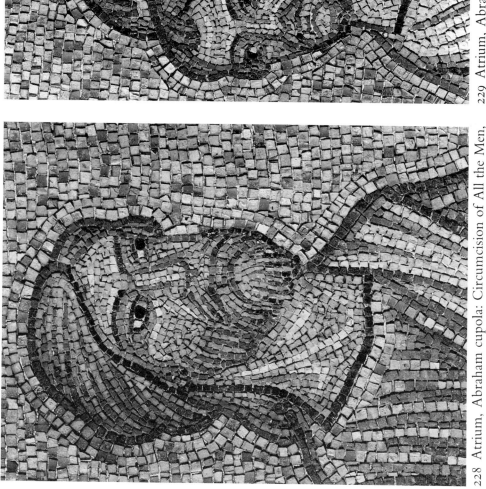

229 Atrium, Abraham cupola: Circumcision of All the Men, men, busts

230 Atrium, Abraham cupola, east lunette

232 Atrium, Abraham cupola, east lunette: Hospitality of Abraham, Abraham

231 Atrium, Abraham cupola, east lunette, Abraham Meeting the Angels, Abraham, bust

233   Atrium, Abraham cupola, east lunette: Abraham Meeting the Angels

234 Atrium, Abraham cupola, west lunette: Circumcision of Isaac

236 Atrium, Abraham cupola: Daniel (*Böhm*)

235 Atrium, Abraham cupola: Jeremiah (*Böhm*)

238 Atrium, Abraham cupola: Ezekiel (*Böhm*)

237 Atrium, Abraham cupola: Isaiah (*Böhm*)

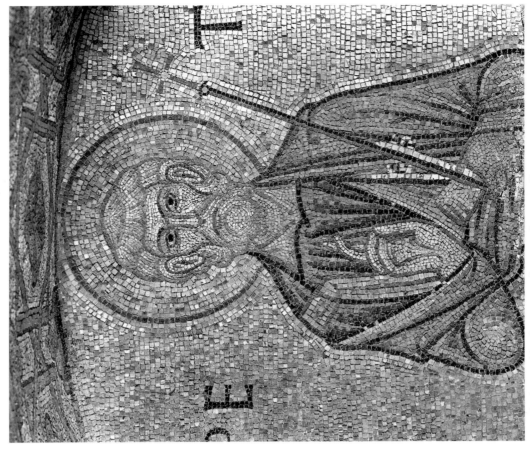

240 Atrium, Abraham cupola, east lunette: Peter

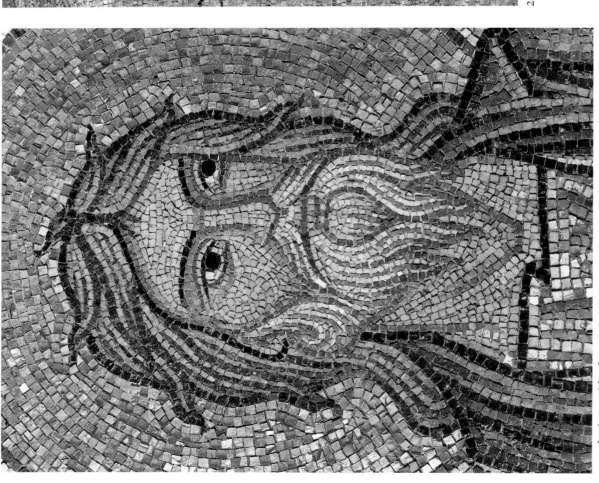

239 Atrium, Abraham cupola: Isaiah, head

242 Atrium, Abraham cupola, central medallion

241 Atrium, Abraham cupola, west lunette, soffit of framing arch: ornament (*Procuratoria*)

243 Atrium, first Joseph cupola, southeast corner (*Strempel*)

244 Atrium, first Joseph cupola, view from below

245 Atrium, first Joseph cupola: Joseph's Dreams of the Sheaves and the Stars

246 Atrium, first Joseph cupola: Joseph Telling His Dream to His Brethren

247 Atrium, first Joseph cupola: Joseph Telling His Dream to His Father and Brethren

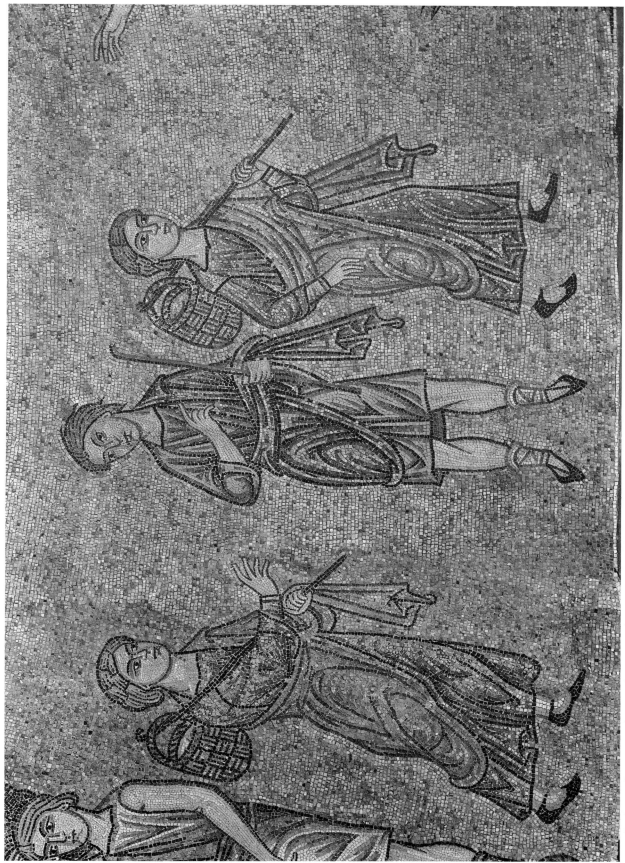

248 Atrium, first Joseph cupola: Man Showing Joseph the Way to Dothan

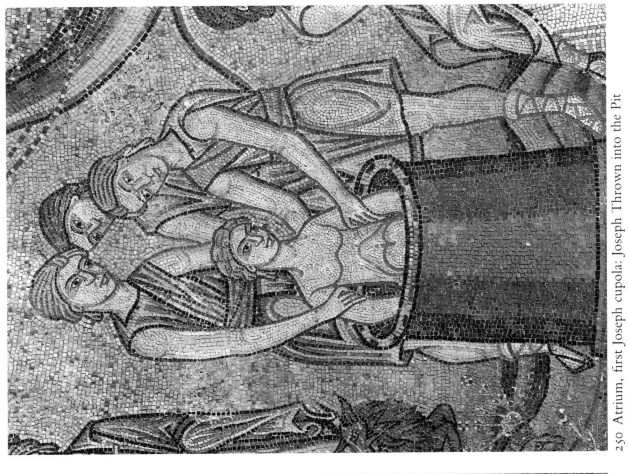

250 Atrium, first Joseph cupola: Joseph Thrown into the Pit

249 Atrium, first Joseph cupola: Brethren Seeing Joseph Coming

251 Atrium, first Joseph cupola: Joseph Thrown into the Pit, the Brethren Feasting

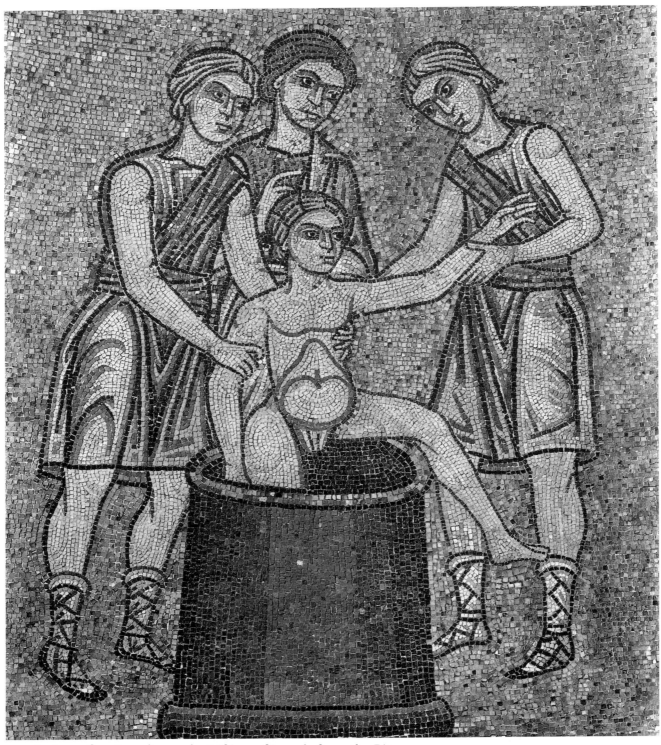

252 Atrium, first Joseph cupola: Lifting of Joseph from the Pit

253 Atrium, first Joseph cupola: Joseph Sold to the Midianites

254 Atrium, first Joseph cupola: Midianites Bring Joseph to Egypt

255 Atrium. first Joseph cupola: Reuben Returning to the Pit

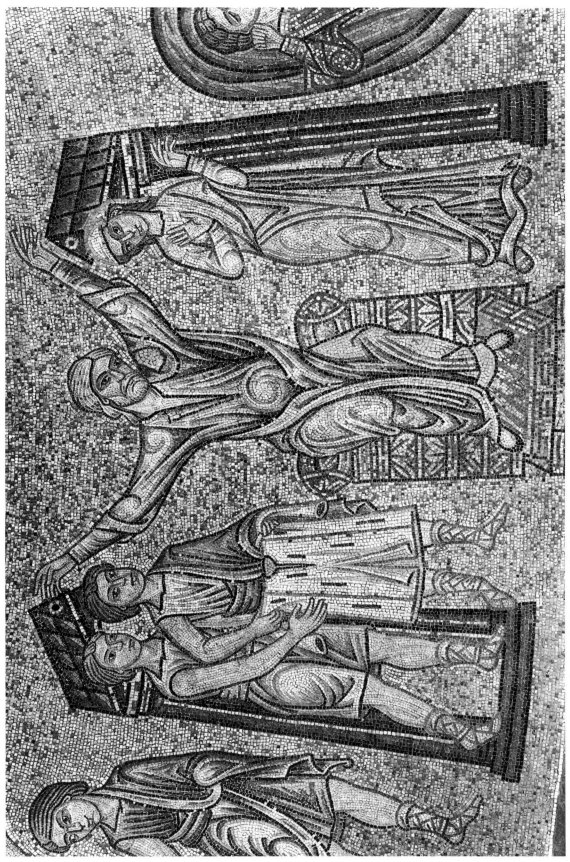

256 Atrium, first Joseph cupola: Jacob Rending His Clothes

258 Atrium, first Joseph cupola: Habakkuk

257 Atrium, first Joseph cupola: Jacob Rending His Clothes, Jacob, head

260 Atrium, first Joseph cupola: Samuel

259 Atrium, first Joseph cupola: Ely

262 Atrium, first Joseph cupola: central medallion

261 Atrium, first Joseph cupola, west lunette: two birds in a tree

263 Atrium, first Joseph cupola, south arch (*Böhm*)

264 Atrium, second Joseph cupola, view from below

265 Atrium, second Joseph cupola: Joseph Sold to Potiphar

266 Atrium, second Joseph cupola: Potiphar Making Joseph Overseer

268 Atrium, second Joseph cupola: Potiphar's Wife Catches Joseph's Garment

267 Atrium, second Joseph cupola: Potiphar's Wife Casting Eyes upon Joseph

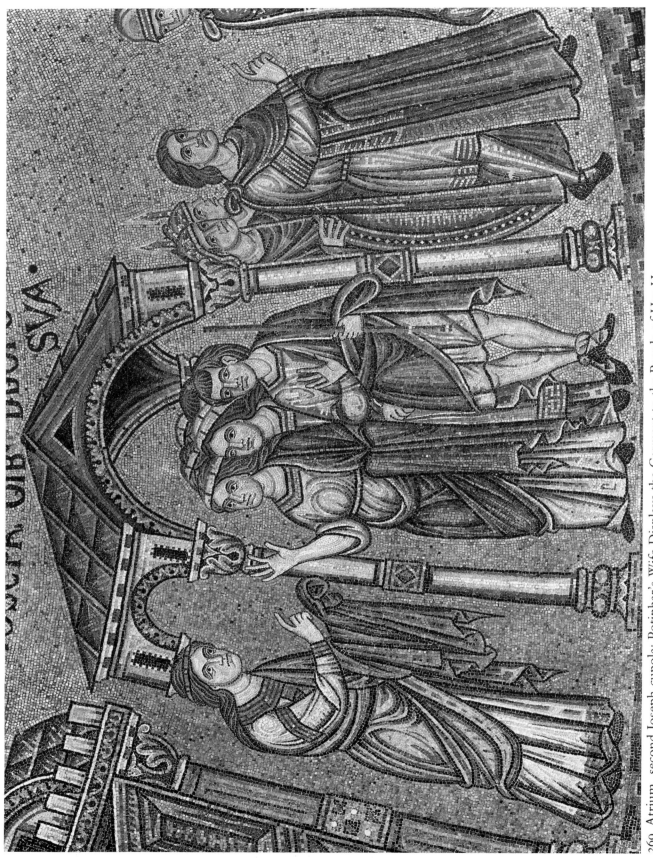

269 Atrium, second Joseph cupola: Potiphar's Wife Displays the Garment to the People of Her House

270 Atrium, second Joseph cupola: Joseph Thrown into Prison

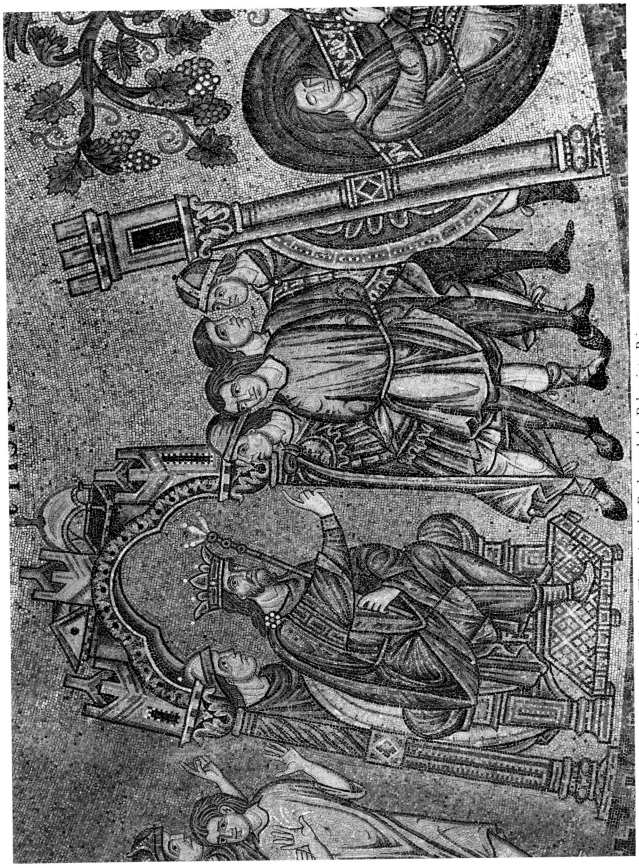

271 Atrium, second Joseph cupola: Pharaoh Throwing the Butler and the Baker into Prison

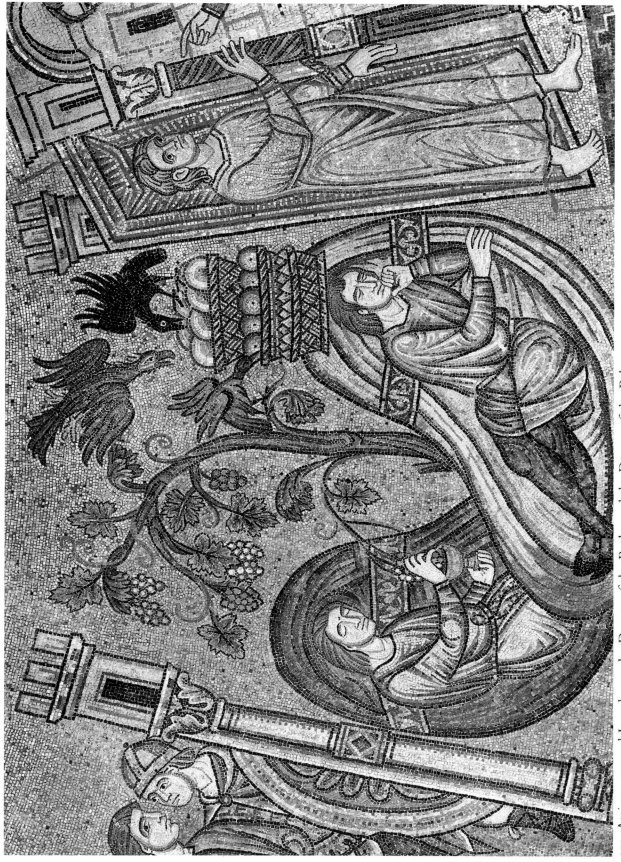

272 Atrium, second Joseph cupola: Dream of the Butler and the Dream of the Baker

273 Atrium, second Joseph cupola: Joseph Interprets the Dreams of the Butler and the Baker

274 Atrium, second Joseph cupola: Joseph Thrown into Prison, Joseph, guards, busts

275 Atrium, second Joseph cupola: Joseph Interprets the Dreams of the Butler and the Baker, Joseph, bust

276 Atrium, second Joseph cupola: Potiphar Making Joseph Overseer, Potiphar's wife, bust

277 Atrium, second Joseph cupola: Potiphar Making Joseph Overseer, Potiphar, head

278 Atrium, second Joseph cupola: Dream of the Butler and the Dream of the Baker, baker, head

279 Atrium, second Joseph cupola: Butler Serving Pharaoh

ORÉM FÉ CIT SVPÉ

280 Atrium, second Joseph cupola: Baker Crucified

281 Atrium, second Joseph cupola: Pharaoh's Dream of the Seven Fat and Lean Kine

282 Atrium, second Joseph cupola: central medallion

284 Atrium, second Joseph cupola, east arch: Sylvester, Agnes (*Alinari*)

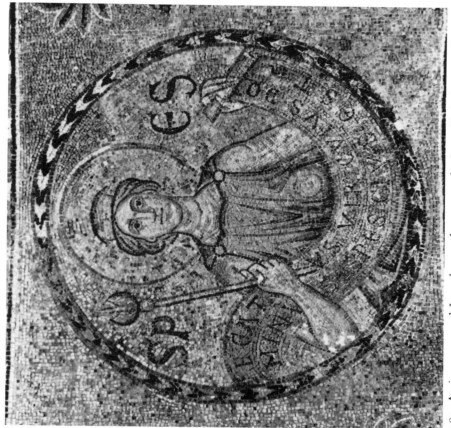

283 Atrium, second Joseph cupola: east arch: Spes (*Böhm*)

HIC PK ARAO PISTOREM FE
HIC PK ARAO PISTOREM SUSP
PINGERNA TOFFICIO SUO
EORNOSA PALIAS SEPTE SPICA ENIE EVACUAS DEVORAVERVT PRIORES PLENAS
PISTOT EVE TI SOPNIOR
HIC PINCERNA DICIT
ET OVALIT IOSEPH DIXAT SIBI
SOPNIOR ASAPIETIB
HIC PINCER NA QVRIT INTERPRE TIQNEM
HIC VIDIT P SOPNIV SEPTE SPICA ICVLNOVOMERABAS
HIC PK ARAO QVIT SEPTE SPICAT CVM VOLVERAT

286 Atrium, second Joseph cupola, south lunette: Pharaoh's Dream of the Seven Ears of Corn

288 Atrium, second Joseph cupola, south lunette: Pharaoh and the Egyptian Magicians, right half

287 Atrium, second Joseph cupola, south lunette: Pharaoh and the Egyptian Magicians, left half

· hIC · PINCERNA DICIT
QVALIT IOSEPh DIXAT SIB

289 Atrium, second Joseph cupola, south lunette: Butler before Pharaoh

290 Atrium, third Joseph cupola, view from below

291 Atrium, third Joseph cupola: Joseph Gathering Corn

292   Atrium, third Joseph cupola: Birth of Manasseh and Ephraim

293 Atrium, third Joseph cupola: Egyptians Crying for Bread

294 Atrium, third Joseph cupola: Egyptians Crying for Bread, Joseph, guards at left, heads

295 Atrium, third Joseph cupola: Joseph Selling Corn

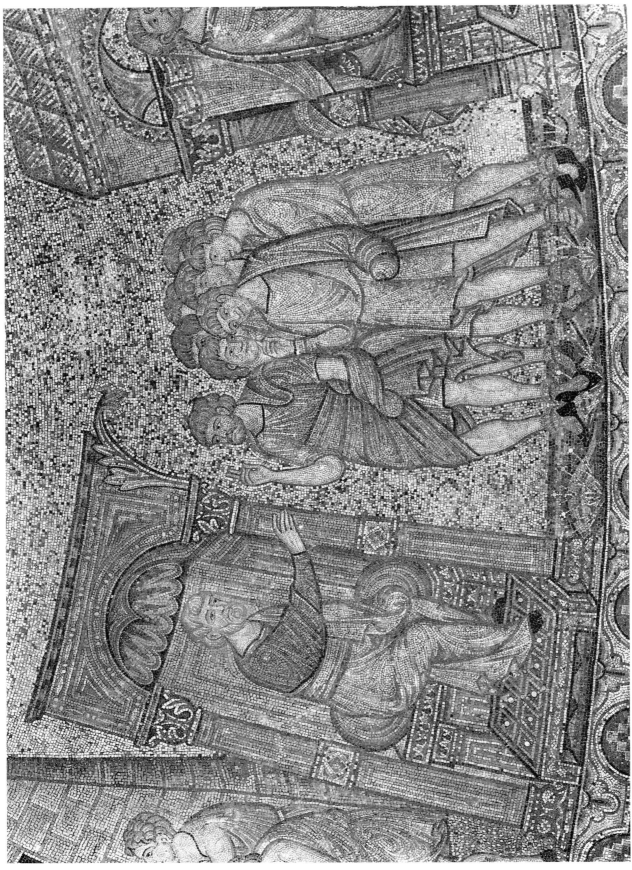

296 Atrium, third Joseph cupola: Jacob Sending His Sons to Egypt

297 Atrium, third Joseph cupola: Joseph Ordering One of the Brethren to Be Bound

298 Atrium, third Joseph cupola: Joseph Turning around and Weeping

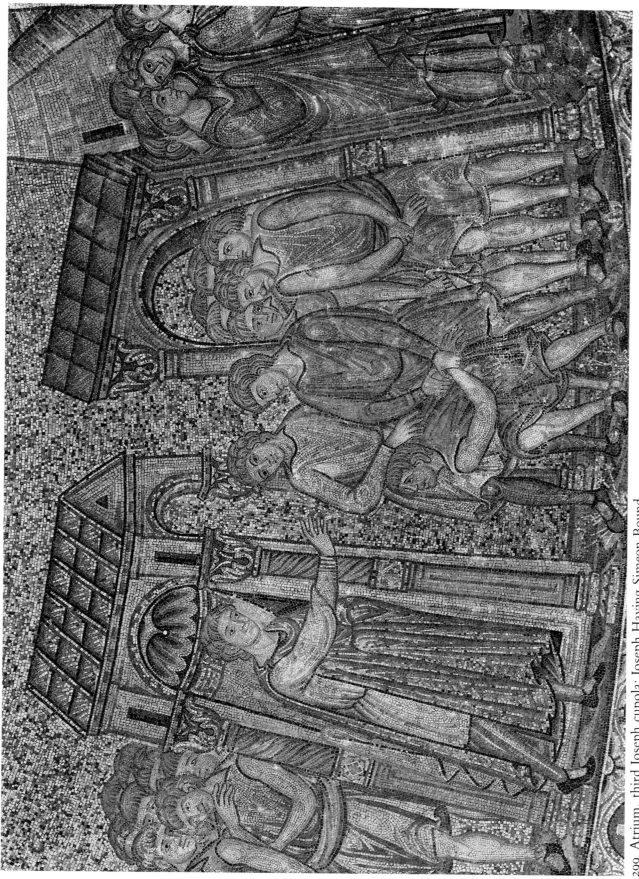

299 Atrium, third Joseph cupola: Joseph Having Simeon Bound

300 Atrium, third Joseph cupola, south lunette

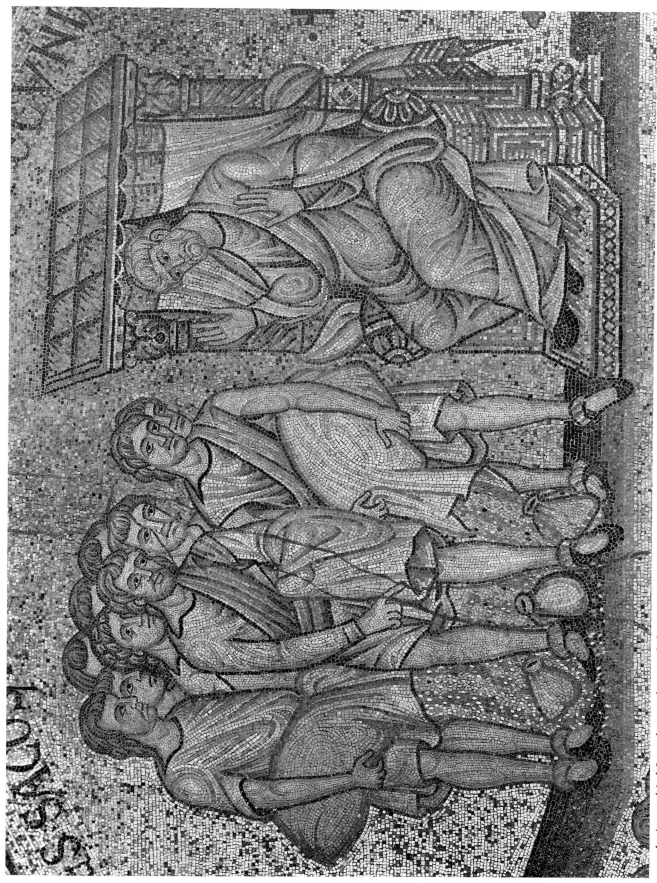

301 Atrium, third Joseph cupola, south lunette: Emptying of the Sacks before Jacob

302 Atrium, third Joseph cupola, south lunette: Emptying of the Sacks before Jacob, brethren, heads and upper bodies

303 Atrium, third Joseph cupola, south lunette: Joseph Giving Benjamin to His Sons

304 Atrium, third Joseph cupola, south lunette: Brethren Load Their Asses

305 Atrium, third Joseph cupola, south lunette: Brethren Brought into Joseph's House

306 Atrium, third Joseph cupola, east arch: Dominic, Nicholas (*Böhm*)

307 Atrium, third Joseph cupola, east arch: Peter Martyr, Blaise (*Böhm*)

309 Atrium, third Joseph cupola: Mark

308 Atrium, third Joseph cupola: John the Evangelist (*Alinari*)

311 Atrium, third Joseph cupola: Matthew

310 Atrium, third Joseph cupola: Luke

LIBRARY ST. MARY'S COLLEGE

312 Atrium, Moses cupola, view from below

313 Atrium, Moses cupola: the Basket Put into and Taken out of the River, Moses Presented to Pharaoh's Daughter, Moses before Pharaoh

314 Atrium, Moses cupola: Moses before Pharaoh

315 Atrium, Moses cupola: Moses Presented to Pharaoh's Daughter, upper part

316 Atrium, Moses cupola: Moses before Pharaoh, Pharaoh and attendants, busts

317 Atrium, Moses cupola: Egyptian Maltreating an Old Hebrew, Moses Looking Around, Moses Slaying the Egyptian

319 Atrium, Moses cupola: Moses Looking Around, Moses Slaying the Egyptian

318 Atrium, Moses cupola: Egyptian Maltreating an Old Hebrew

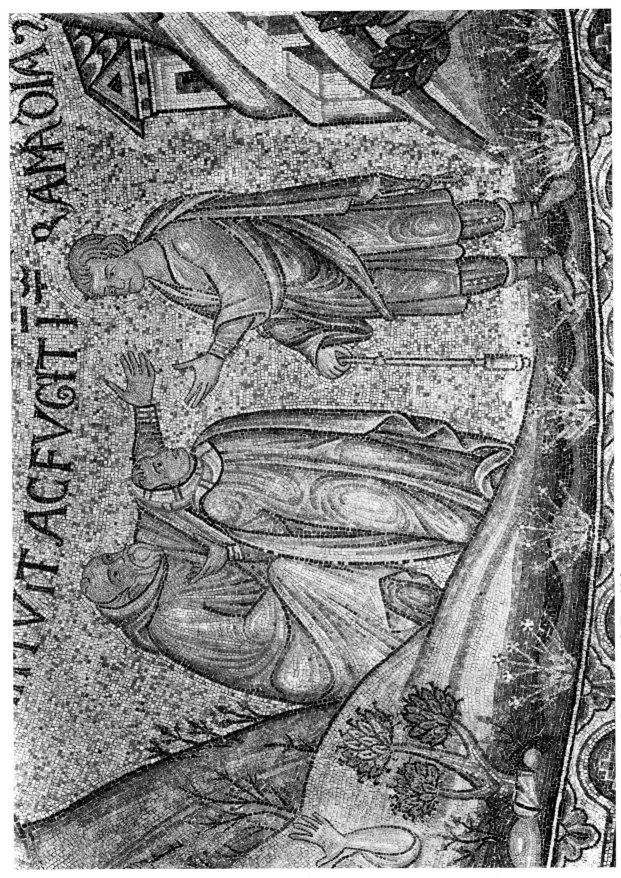

320 Atrium, Moses cupola: Moses with Two Hebrews

321 Atrium, Moses cupola: Moses Wandering, Moses at the Well

322 Atrium, Moses cupola: Moses and the Daughters of Jethro at the Well

323 Atrium, Moses cupola: Moses Driving away the Shepherds

325 Atrium, Moses cupola: Moses Driving away the Shepherds, Moses, bust

324 Atrium, Moses cupola: Moses and the Daughters of Jethro at the Well, daughter at right, bust

327 Atrium, Moses cupola: Moses Received by Jethro, Jethro, bust

326 Atrium, Moses cupola: Moses Driving away the Shepherds, Shepherd at left, bust

328 Atrium, Moses cupola: Moses Received by Jethro

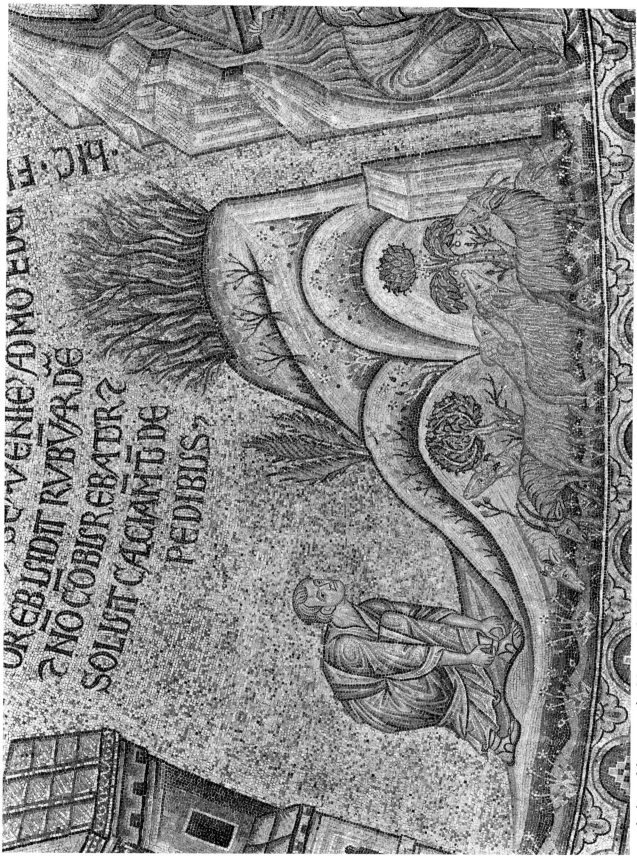

329 Atrium, Moses cupola: Moses at the Burning Bush

330 Atrium, Moses cupola, north apse: Desert Miracles of Moses

331 Atrium, Moses cupola, north apse: Miracle of the Manna, Miracle of the Quails (*Böhm*)

333 Atrium, Moses cupola: Solomon

332 Atrium, Moses cupola: David

335 Atrium, Moses cupola: central medallion

334 Atrium, Moses cupola: Malachi

336 Cappella Zen, vault, view from below (*Alinari*)

337 Cappella Zen, vault, east half

338 Cappella Zen, vault, west half

+ SCS MAC ROGAT A FRARIB; SCRISIT SCS PE RAP BA EVAGLM SCI MACI
EVANGLIVM
RADITEC
LEGED

+ CIS NISI TFACET P MARE UBI N SCPO TECCLIA BEAT PERVS COFERT S OR
S MAC ANGLS EINS CAS IT P POST ALIVS ATS PSAM.
PATRCHAT

339 Cappella Zen, vault, east half: Mark Writing the Gospel, Mark Presenting the Gospel to Peter

ADRIA PERGIT NAVGIO ALEXADRIA RADIT CALIA M VRVP BS UT OI P OC VS B RE
RAVIT MANS SAP S MARC SANAV

HIC CAE NATVS RAHTBR AD LOCA BVEISL SEPELTR BEAT MARCS

340 Cappella Zen, vault, west half: Mark Sailing to Alexandria, Mark Healing Anianus (*Alinari*)

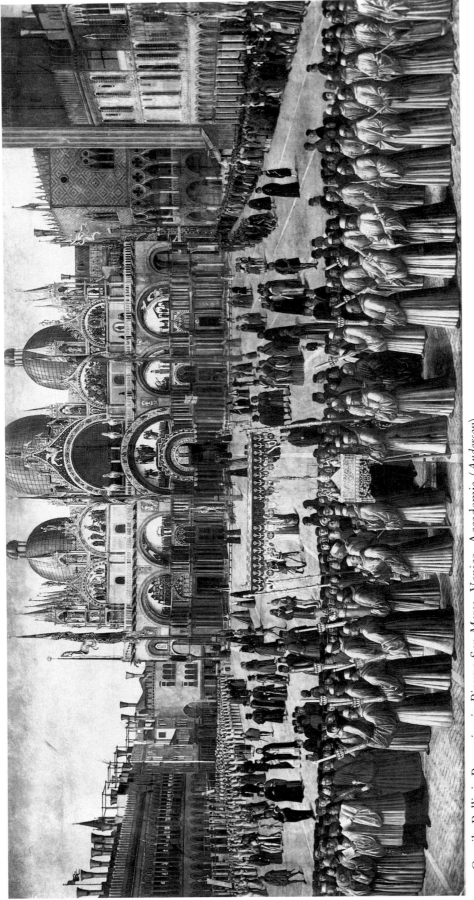

341 Gentile Bellini: *Procession in Piazza San Marco*, Venice, Accademia (*Anderson*)

342 Façade: Second Coming of Christ, after Bellini (*Böhm*)

343 Façade: Deposition, after Bellini (*Böhm*)

344 Façade: Anastasis, after Bellini (*Böhm*)

345 Façade: Resurrection, after Bellini (*Böhm*)

346 Façade: Ascension, after Bellini (*Böhm*)

347 Façade: Mark's Relics Taken from His Tomb, after Bellini (*Böhm*)

348 Façade: Mark's Relics Shipped to Venice, after Bellini (*Böhm*)

349 Façade: Mark's Relics Received in Venice, after Bellini (*Böhm*)

350 Façade: Mark's Relics Transferred into Church, after Bellini (*Böhm*)

351 Façade (Porta Sant'Alipio): Mark's Relics Transferred into Church (*Alinari*)

352 Façade (Porta Sant'Alipio): Mark's Relics Transferred into Church, church, upper part (*Böhm*)

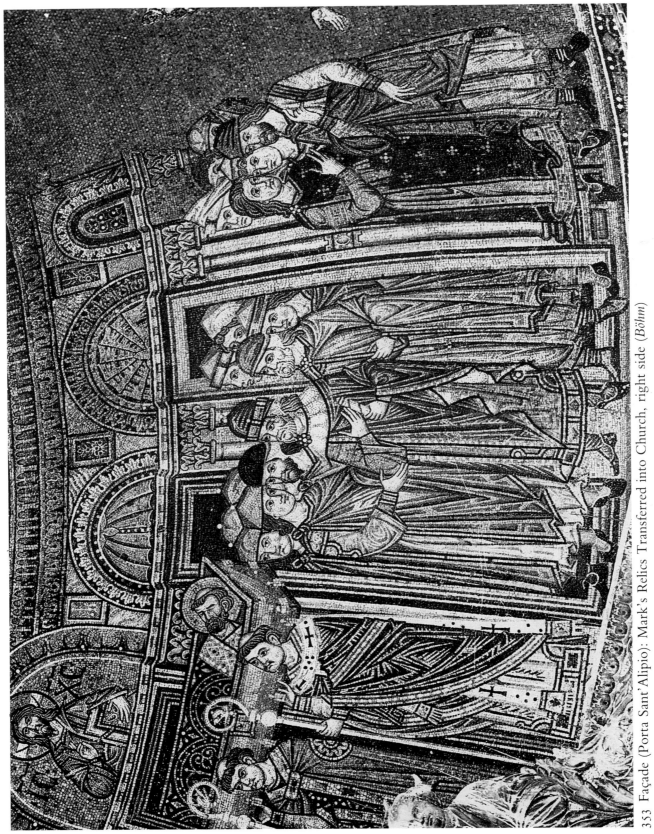

353 Façade (Porta Sant'Alipio): Mark's Relics Transferred into Church, right side (*Böhm*)

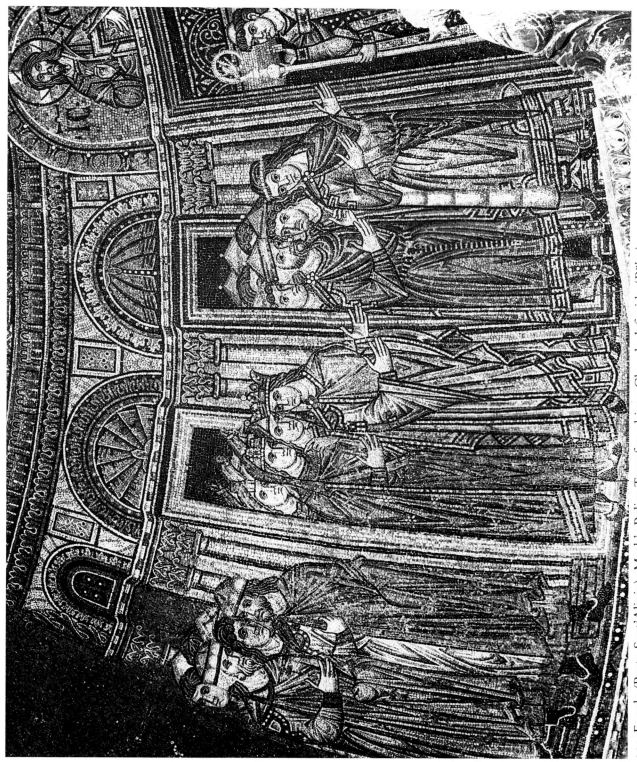

354 Façade (Porta Sant'Alipio): Mark's Relics Transferred into Church, left side (*Böhm*)